The Ultimate WOK COOKBOOK

FOR BEGINNERS

200 Delicious Restaurant Chinese Recipes for Chinese-Foods Lovers to
Stir-Fry and Steam at Home

Teresa Parker

Content

Chapter 5: Grain and Rice 23

Chapter 6: Pasta 28

Chapter 7: Fish and Seafood 35

Introduction

Wok, it is not just a pan! It signifies the rich Chinese culinary tradition and culture that we all love to enjoy. Be its authentic dim sims or stir-fries; Wok is used to make a variety of Chinese recipes in amazingly delicious ways. The uses of Wok are many, so much so that you can create an entire menu out of a Wok. You just need to pick up the right ingredients, get the suitable essentials, and get started. But wait! Wok cooking is almost impossible without having a list of the easy recipe, to begin with. Here comes this cookbook with an extensive collection of Chinese Wok recipes that will leave you spellbound with their great taste and aroma.

Chapter 1: Understanding Wok Cooking

Wok is a deep round-bottomed cooking pot, which has become more than just a utensil in Chinese cooking; it has rather become its symbol. The most typical usage of a Wok is stir-frying, although it may also be used for a variety of other things because of its distinctive form. Because it is so deep, food can be boiled in it or deep-fried in it by filling it with oil. It can also be used to steam fish or vegetables if it has a lid.

The Magic of Wok Cooking

A Wok is essentially a frying pan with a curved base, which deeply affects how your food is cooked. It is a healthier cooking option due to its great heat retention capacity and the fact that it uses very little cooking oil. The food can be pushed against the Wok's sides to allow extra oil to drip off before serving. Because of the high sides, you can cook and stir a lot of food without worrying about it spilling out of the pan or soaking up oil.

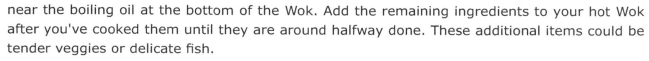

Heat is evenly distributed over a larger surface area in a Wok than it would in a frying pan due to its conical shape. This feature enables even cooking of meat or veggies in a single pan. Things that require longer to cook, such as tougher meat or harder vegetables, should be maintained near the boiling oil at the bottom of the Wok. Add the remaining ingredients to your hot Wok after you've cooked them until they are around halfway done. These additional items could be tender veggies or delicate fish.

A Wok has the advantage of having a larger useful volume than a regular frying pan. Due to the higher edges of the wok you can add bulk of food to cook in it. Therefore, cooking larger quantities of food is simple, and you can have a selection of delicious leftovers for your supper the following day. Plus you won't spill as much food over the pan, keeping your kitchen cleaner because there won't be any leftovers to clean off your burner.

Wok from the Past

Historians and chefs have several theories about Wok's origin. According to others, the Wok's versatility during the Han dynasty's food shortage period allowed a range of meals to be produced with the same materials. There is also a theory that tribes in the distant past needed cooking gear that was both portable and capable of preparing a lot of food rapidly since they had to carry all of their things with them as they traveled across the country. Another hypothesis is that the paucity of fuel and oil during the Han era allowed people to cook food in the Wok using relatively little oil.

Chapter 2: Basics of Wok Cooking

There are several different types of Woks that are available today in the market, and to get the best results, you need to bring the "Right" one to your Kitchen. Once you get that, you can move on to the next steps of wok cookery, which involve setting up a pantry, picking the ingredients, seasoning the wok, and cooking.

The "Right" Wok – Buying the Best

For cooking at home, a great Wok need not be expensive. For less than $40, you can get a good Wok that will last for years or even decades! To get such a wok, you should consider the following few important points:

- **Carbon steel is a quality material for a home-use Wok.** It is thin, evenly distributes heat, and produces a naturally non-stick surface with usage and seasoning.

- **Use a Wok that has a flat-round bottom and flat sides.** The number of ingredients that you can fit on that hot section of the pan will be increased thanks to the flat surface. You may have seen circular Woks used to cook street food in Thailand or in restaurant kitchens, but domestic ranges do not burn hot enough to cook in these rounded Woks.

- **12 to 14 inches Sizes:** This size appears to be the ideal one for cooking with a Wok at home. A supper for around 4 people can be prepared on a 12 or 14-inch Wok (measured at the widest area of the pan), which is still manageable in size.

- **Any Wok you purchase should have two handles.** Some Woks have symmetrical, brief handles on either side (Cantonese-style). Some have a long handle and a short handle. The pan's small handle makes it simple to pick up, and its long handle makes it simple to shake the pan while cooking (while keeping your hands away from the heat). The most useful Woks for home cooking, in my opinion, are those with one short handle and one long handle, but this depends on the individual.

Kitchen Essentials for Everyday Chinese Cooking

If you are a Chinese food lover who does not enjoy Chinese takeout, then you need to set up a Kitchen filled with the essentials required to make delicious Chinese food. Besides a good Wok, here is what you need to have in the Kitchen.

A Cleaver: The shape of a Chinese cleaver is rectangular. It has a thick, hefty handle made of wood, plastic, or stainless steel. It is used to sever bone. Chinese cooks make use of cleavers for slicing un-boned or boneless meat, mincing, dicing, chopping vegetables, and cutting vegetables into delicate, artistic shapes. They also use them to smash garlic or ginger.

A Cutting Board: Cutting meat and chopping vegetables on a cutting board protects the work surface. Cutting boards come in three different varieties: acrylic, bamboo, and wooden. The ideal ones are made of acrylic or wood.

A 'Wok Shovel': Chinese cuisine requires a decent "Wok shovel", which is a necessity. It's more than just a turner or a spatula. The best utensil for most stir-fries is a Wok shovel, which is made specifically for Wok stir-frying and scooping. The front of the tiny shovel's rounded edge fits the Wok's curve perfectly. Having a tool that effectively removes the rest of the scrumptious food from the Wok's bottom is really convenient. Larger amounts of food can be stirred and tossed with a Wok shovel.

A Chinese Scoop Strainer: In China, straining, skimming, and deep-frying are all done with a scoop strainer. Lifting fried fish, chunks of meat, and chips out of hot oil or noodles, wontons, and dumplings out of boiling water are both highly practical. There are various sizes available. For domestic use, a diameter of 15 cm (6 inches) is most typical.

A Ladle: To transfer soup or stew from a pot or Wok to a bowl, use a ladle. They can be made out of wood, plastic, aluminum, bamboo, stainless steel, silver, and other materials.

Long Chopsticks: Using cooking chopsticks, you can fish noodles and other food items that are difficult to scrape out of a boiling pan or skillet. They are longer (30+ cm, 12+") than those used for eating. In the Kitchen, regular chopsticks are used for stir-frying, beating eggs, and combining ingredients.

Steaming Baskets: In China, not everything is stir-fried. Cooking in China frequently involves the use of steaming baskets. All types of cuisine, including dumplings, buns, fish, pancakes, meat, and vegetables, are steamed using them. They enable multi-dish preparation by stacking these tray-like baskets several layers high. They come in various sizes and are frequently used with a Wok.

Getting Started with Wok Cookery

If you've ever observed someone using a Wok in a commercial kitchen, you could have seen them combining all the ingredients in the Wok, tossing it around, and then transferring it to a dish. Those chefs frequently use extremely hot burners and Woks, maybe far hotter than you will ever experience at home. Fortunately, there is a simple technique to ensure that everything in your home kitchen cooks correctly.

Step 1: Set your Wok over a medium-high heat source to begin. Add roughly a tablespoon of cooking oil to the hot Wok, then rotate or swirl the Wok to evenly distribute the hot oil over the bottom and edges.

Step 2: Use paper towels to dry the protein like meat, poultry, tofu, or seafood. Protein that is dry will sear more easily. For proteins that aren't completely dry, steam rather than sear. Add your preferred protein—chicken, beef, pork, shrimp, tofu, etc.—in a single layer to the heated oil. For a few minutes, don't stir the protein; instead, wait for it to sear on the bottom. Flip the protein over with a spatula to brown the other side; a Wok spatula works excellent for this.

Step 3: Give the protein a toss after it has been seared on both sides and continue cooking it until it is almost cooked through. Place the protein on a plate after seasoning it with salt.

Step 4: Add another tablespoon of frying oil and bring the Wok back up to medium-high heat. Toss in aromatics like garlic, onions, ginger, shallots, and chilis. For a minute, cook them while stirring regularly so they can flavor the oil. Vegetables should be added to aromatics in descending order of cooking time. For instance:

- 6-7 minutes (hard vegetables) for potatoes, brussels sprouts, carrots, broccoli, cauliflower, and 4 to 5 minutes (medium-hard vegetables), such as zucchini and mushrooms.
- For medium-soft veggies, cook for 3 to 4 minutes: bell peppers, snow peas, and baby carrots.
- 1-2 minutes (soft vegetables): peas, maize kernels, tomatoes, and leafy greens.

All vegetables should be cooked with continuous stirring. If you're feeling bold, you may also shake the Wok back and forth or use it to fling the vegetables a few inches into the air! Add about a tablespoon of water if the Wok appears dry while cooking the veggies or if they begin to burn before they are fully cooked. If you use this method with vegetables that take longer to cook, you can cover the Wok with a lid after you've added the water. The vegetables will steam.

Step 5: Add the protein back to the pan after the vegetables have all been cooked until they are fork-tender. Then, pour the sauce or liquids down the sides of the Wok. The liquids can be heated up before they reach the other components by being poured down the sides. Include them now as well if you're cooking fried rice or another grain. Before adding any grain or rice to the Wok, make sure it has been precooked and is soft. Toss everything together until the protein is fully cooked and the dish is sauce-coated.

Seasoning Tips

Seasoning helps cover the surface of wok and make it non-stick. A protective coating called Patina is formed over the surface every time you oil the Wok's surface and heat it for cooking. The coating helps to prevent corrosion and rust while enhancing the flavor of the food cooked in your Wok. The Patina builds up heavier and thicker each time you use your Wok for cooking with oil, creating a naturally non-stick surface. It is essential to season a fresh Wok for the first time before cooking anything.

1. If your wok is new then wash it first and place over high heat. Add splash of water and let them evaporate to water the cooking surface of the wok. Then remove this wok from the heat and allow it to cool down.

2. Apply oil to the Wok. Once your Wok is cool enough to handle, coat the inside and exterior with a very thin layer of seasoning oil using a paper towel or soft kitchen towel. Use only a high smoke point cooking oil, such as peanut, canola, grapeseed, or vegetable oil, which can sustain high heat of 450 degrees Fahrenheit or more.

3. Heat the Wok again. Put the greased Wok back on the fire and raise the heat to

medium-high until the smoking stops. To ensure that every section of the Wok reaches a smoking point and then stops smoking, move the Wok all the way around the burner. When the surface has been sufficiently seasoned, it acquires a matte finish and a dark tone. Wash and rinse the Wok with hot water and a Wok brush. Without removing any of the flavors, this cleans the Wok.

4. Put the Wok back on the stove over high heat to get rid of any leftover water from the rinsing operation. The Wok is now ready for use, but if you want a better non-stick surface and a stronger protective coating, repeat the previous processes one to two more times.

How to Care for a Seasoned Wok

A seasoned Wok is a relatively delicate piece of cookware that requires some special handling. Follow these guidelines to maintain a cast-iron or carbon-steel Wok:

- Do not use soap. Avoid using dish soap or any other sudsy cleaner while cleaning the Wok. The nice Patina, which may have developed over many years in the case of an older Wok, is removed by soap.

- Use the Wok frequently to cook. To consistently season the pan, fill a weekly meal plan with Asian recipes like stir-fries, scallion noodles, or orange chicken. The Wok is re'seasoned each time you add oil to the pan and heat it up for cooking.

- After cleaning the Wok with water, be sure to completely dry it. To get rid of any leftover water, either wipe the Wok with a clean, dry kitchen towel or heat it up on the burner over medium or high heat.

- Select soft sponges. If there are food particles attached to the Wok, briefly dip it into boiling water, take it out, then scrub it with a soft sponge. Scratching the Wok with abrasive sponges, such as scouring pads or a steel scrubber, will remove the seasoning and Patina that have accumulated over time. The accumulation shields the Wok and keeps food from sticking.

- Avoid using sharp-edged spoons or spatulas while cooking in a wok, as they scratch the Patina developed on its surface.

Conclusion

Your Wok cooking journey starts now! It's time to stop ordering tasteless Chinese takeouts and cook some authentic Chinese Wok recipes. With the wide-ranging collection of Wok recipes in this book, you can definitely make a delicious menu of your own. Pick and choose your favorite recipes, select the right Wok and perfect combination of ingredients, then just get started, and you will end up serving the best Chinese meal at the table.

Teriyaki Tofu with Mushroom, page 8

Stir-Fried Sweet Snow Peas, page 16

Classic Korean Vegetables with Gochujang, page 11

Garlic Eggs and Bok Choy, page 13

Chapter 3: Vegetables and Sides

Chili Myanmarese Vegetables

Prep Time: 9 minutes, Cook Time: 5 minutes, Serves: 4

INGREDIENTS:

1 medium carrot, roll-cut into ½-inch pieces
2 cups sugar snap or snow pea pods
1 small mango, peeled and cut into ½-inch pieces
2 baby bok choy, leaves separated
2 to 3 red chiles, cut into ¼-inch pieces
1 red bell pepper, cut into 1-inch pieces
2 garlic cloves, crushed and chopped
Juice of 1 lime
2 tbsps. cooking oil
1 tbsp. fish sauce
1 tbsp. Chinese five-spice powder
1 tsp. hot sesame oil

DIRECTIONS:

1. Whisk together the sesame oil, lime juice, fish sauce, and five-spice powder in a small bowl. Set aside.
2. In a wok, heat the cooking oil over high heat until it shimmers.
3. Add the garlic and carrot and stir-fry for 1 minute.
4. Place the chiles and stir-fry for 30 seconds.
5. Then toss the pea pods, bell pepper and mango and stir-fry for 1 minute.
6. Pour the sesame oil mixture and the bok choy and stir-fry for 1 minute.
7. Serve hot.

Teriyaki Tofu with Mushroom

Prep Time: 11 minutes, Cook Time: 6 minutes, Serves: 5

INGREDIENTS:

1 pound (454 g) extra-firm tofu, drained and cut into 1-inch cubes
4 ounces (113 g) shiitake mushrooms, cut into slices
1 medium onion, cut into 1-inch pieces
1 red bell pepper, cut into 1-inch pieces
2 garlic cloves, crushed and chopped
¼ cup plus 2 tbsps.
tamari, divided
2 tbsps. toasted sesame seeds
2 tbsps. mirin wine
2 tbsps. rice vinegar
2 tbsps. toasted sesame oil
2 tbsps. brown sugar
2 tbsps. cooking oil
1 tbsp. ginger, crushed and chopped
1 tbsp. white miso
1 tbsp. cornstarch

DIRECTIONS:

1. Whisk together ¼ cup of the tamari, the mirin, rice vinegar, sesame oil, brown sugar, miso, and cornstarch in a small bowl. Set aside.
2. In a wok, heat the cooking oil over high heat until it shimmers.
3. Add the tofu, ginger, garlic and remaining 2 tbsps. of tamari and stir-fry for 2 minutes, or until the tofu starts to brown.
4. Put the onion and stir-fry for 1 minute.
5. Place the bell pepper and mushrooms and stir-fry for 1 minute.
6. Pour the tamari mixture to the wok and stir-fry until a light glaze forms.
7. Sprinkle with the sesame seeds and serve hot.

Delicious Stir-Fried Broccoli and Bamboo Shoots

Prep Time: 5 minutes, Cook Time: 5 minutes, Serves: 4

INGREDIENTS:

4 cups broccoli florets
1 (8-ounce / 227-g) can sliced bamboo shoots, rinsed and drained
1 peeled fresh ginger slice, about the size of a quarter
2 garlic cloves, minced
2 tbsps. vegetable oil
2 tbsps. water
2 tsps. toasted sesame seeds
1 tbsp. light soy sauce
1 tsp. sesame oil
Kosher salt

DIRECTIONS:

1. Heat a wok over high heat until a drop of water sizzles and evaporates on contact. Add the vegetable oil and swirl to coat the base of the wok well. Season the oil with the ginger slice and a pinch of salt. Let the ginger to sizzle in the oil for about 30 seconds, swirling slowly.
2. Place the broccoli and stir-fry for 2 minutes until bright green. Pour the water and cover the pan for 2 minutes to steam the broccoli.
3. Take the cover, put the garlic and continue stir-frying for 30 seconds. Toss in the bamboo shoots and continue to stir-fry for an additional 30 seconds.
4. Pour the light soy and sesame oil. Transfer to a heated platter and discard the ginger. Garnish with sesame seeds and serve.

Thai-Style Stir-Fried Vegetables

Prep Time: 10 minutes, Cook Time: 5 minutes, Serves: 4

INGREDIENTS:

2 cups sugar snap or snow pea pods
2 cups basil leaves
1 medium carrot, roll-cut into ½-inch pieces
1 medium onion, cut into 1-inch pieces
1 cup fresh bean sprouts
1 red bell pepper, cut into 1-inch pieces
½ cup chopped cilantro

2 garlic cloves, crushed and chopped
3 tbsps. brown sugar
2 tbsps. cooking oil
2 tbsps. red Thai curry paste
2 tbsps. fish sauce
Juice of 1 lime
1 tbsp. cornstarch
1 tsp. hot sesame oil

DIRECTIONS:

1. Whisk together the curry paste, fish sauce, sesame oil, lime juice, brown sugar and cornstarch in a small bowl. Set aside.
2. In a wok, heat the cooking oil over high heat until it shimmers.
3. Add the garlic and carrot and stir-fry for 1 minute.
4. Then place the onion and stir-fry for 1 minute.
5. Toss the pea pods and bell pepper and stir-fry for 1 minute.
6. Pour the curry paste mixture and stir until it forms a glaze.
7. Put the basil and toss for 30 seconds until it wilts.
8. Top with the bean sprouts and cilantro and serve.

Steamed Tofu

Prep Time: 5 minutes, Cook Time: 15 minutes, Serves: 4

INGREDIENTS:

1 pound (454 g) medium tofu
2 garlic cloves, finely minced
2 scallions, thinly sliced
2 tbsps. light soy sauce
1 tbsp. sesame oil

1 tbsp. coarsely chopped fresh cilantro leaves
2 tsps. black vinegar
1 tsp. peeled finely minced fresh ginger
½ tsp. sugar

DIRECTIONS:

1. Take the tofu from its packaging, being careful to keep it intact. Put it on a large plate and carefully slice it into 1- to 1½-inch-thick slices. Set aside for 5 minutes. Resting the tofu allows more of its whey to drain out.
2. Rinse a bamboo steamer basket and its lid with cold water and place it in the wok. Add about 2 inches of cold water, or until it reaches above the bottom rim of the steamer by about ¼ to ½ inch, but not so high that the water touches the bottom of the basket.
3. Drain any extra whey from the tofu plate and arrange the plate in the bamboo steamer. Cover the lid and set the wok over medium-high heat. Bring the water to a boil and steam the tofu for about 6 to 8 minutes.
4. When the tofu is steaming, in a small saucepan, stir the light soy, garlic, ginger, sesame oil, vinegar, and sugar together over low heat until the sugar is dissolved entirely.
5. Pour the warm sauce over the tofu and garnish with the scallions and cilantro. Serve hot.

Classic Buddha's Delight

Prep Time: 20 minutes, Cook Time: 30 minutes, Serves: 4

INGREDIENTS:

1 delicata squash, halved, seeded, and cut into bite-size pieces
1 cup sugar snap peas, strings removed
1 (8-ounce / 227-g) can water chestnuts, rinsed and drained
Small handful (about ⅓ cup) dried wood ear mushrooms
2 peeled fresh ginger slices, each about the

size of a quarter
8 dried shiitake mushrooms
2 tbsps. vegetable oil
2 tbsps. Shaoxing rice wine
2 tbsps. light soy sauce
2 tsps. sugar
1 tsp. sesame oil
Kosher salt
Freshly ground black pepper

DIRECTIONS:

1. Soak the dried mushrooms in two bowls just covered with hot water until softened, about 20 minutes. Drain and discard the wood ear soaking liquid. Drain and reserve ½ cup of the shiitake liquid. Add the light soy, sugar and sesame oil to the mushroom liquid and stir to dissolve the sugar. Set aside.
2. Heat a wok over high heat until a drop of water sizzles and evaporates on contact. Add the vegetable oil and swirl to coat the base of the wok well. Season the oil with the ginger slices and a pinch of salt. Let the ginger sizzle in the oil for about 30 seconds, swirling slowly.
3. Place the squash and stir-fry, tossing with the seasoned oil for about 3 minutes. Pour both mushrooms and the rice wine and continue to stir-fry for 30 seconds. Put the snow peas and water chestnuts, tossing to coat with oil. Toss the reserved mushroom seasoning liquid and cover. Continue cooking, stirring occasionally, until the vegetables are just tender, about 5 minutes.
4. Uncover the lid and season with salt and pepper to taste. Discard the ginger and serve warm.

Easy Buddha's Delight

Prep Time: 10 minutes, Cook Time: 6 minutes, Serves: 6

INGREDIENTS:

1 pound (454 g) extra-firm tofu, well drained, patted dry, and cut into bite-size pieces	pieces
	3 garlic cloves, crushed and chopped
1 medium carrot, roll-cut into ½-inch pieces	¼ cup cooking oil
	2 tbsps. rice wine
1 dozen sugar snap or snow pea pods	2 tbsps. soy sauce or tamari
4 ounces (113 g) mushrooms, cut into slices	2 tbsps. rice vinegar
	1 tbsp. hot sesame oil
1 red bell pepper, cut into 1-inch pieces	1 tbsp. Chinese five-spice powder
4 scallions, cut into 1-inch	1 tbsp. ginger, crushed and chopped
	1 tbsp. cornstarch

DIRECTIONS:

1. Whisk together the rice wine, soy sauce, rice vinegar, sesame oil, five-spice powder, and cornstarch in a small bowl. Set aside.
2. In a wok, heat the cooking oil over high heat until it shimmers.
3. Add the tofu, garlic and ginger and and stir-fry for 1 minute, or until the tofu begins to brown.
4. Place the carrot, mushrooms and bell pepper and stir-fry for 1 minute.
5. Put the pea pods and stir-fry for 1 minute.
6. Toss the scallions and stir-fry for 30 seconds.
7. Pour the rice wine mixture and stir-fry until a light glaze forms.
8. Serve warm.

Traditional Asian Vegetarian Wok Di San Xian

Prep Time: 20 minutes, Cook Time: 25 minutes, Serves: 6

INGREDIENTS:

1 pound (454 g) potatoes, thickly sliced	Oil, for frying
2 long eggplants	**SAUCE:**
1 green pepper, peeled and chopped into tiny chunks	3 tbsps. water
	2 tbsps. soy sauce
	1 tbsp. cornstarch
½ cup cornstarch	½ tbsp. dark soy sauce
1 green onion, chopped	½ tsp. sugar
2 garlic cloves, chopped	Salt and pepper as per your taste

DIRECTIONS:

1. Soak the eggplants in gently salted water for about 20 minutes.
2. Drain and coat a thin cornstarch to the surface.
3. In a small bowl, mix all of the stir-frying sauce ingredients.
4. Heat the oil to create a 3cm oil layer in the wok.
5. Arrange the potatoes in the pan and heat until they are fully done.
6. Put eggplant and cook it gently until it is completely done.
7. Stir-fry the green pepper for 10 seconds.
8. Then add the green onion and garlic till fragrant.
9. Toss in the stir fry sauce for 30 seconds. Let it boil.
10. Stir all the remaining ingredients and fry until all of the pieces are evenly coated.
11. Serve hot.

Stir-Fried Colorful Vegetable Medley

Prep Time: 6 minutes, Cook Time: 15 minutes, Serves: 4 to 6

INGREDIENTS:

½ white onion, cut into 1-inch pieces	1 small handful green beans, trimmed
1 large carrot, peeled and cut diagonally into ¼-inch-thick slices	1 red bell pepper, cut into 1-inch pieces
6 fresh shiitake mushrooms, stems removed and caps thinly sliced	2 garlic cloves, finely minced
	2 scallions, thinly sliced
2 celery ribs, cut diagonally into ¼-inch-thick slices	1 peeled fresh ginger slice, about the size of a quarter
	3 tbsps. vegetable oil
	Kosher salt

DIRECTIONS:

1. Heat a wok over high heat until a drop of water sizzles and evaporates on contact. Add the oil and swirl to coat the base of the wok well. Season the oil with the ginger slice and a pinch of salt. Allow to sizzle in the oil for about 30 seconds, swirling slowly.
2. Place the carrot, onion and celery to the wok and stir-fry, moving the vegetables around in the wok quickly with a spatula. When the vegetables begin to turn tender, about 4 minutes, put the mushrooms and continue stirring them in the hot wok.
3. When the mushrooms look soft, place the bell pepper and continue to stir, about 4 more minutes. When the bell peppers turn soft, add the green beans and stir until tender, about 3 more minutes. Place the garlic and stir until fragrant.
4. Transfer the vegetables to a platter and discard the ginger. Garnish with the scallions and serve hot.

Classic Korean Vegetables with Gochujang

Prep Time: 7 minutes, Cook Time: 5 minutes, Serves: 4

INGREDIENTS:

2 cups sugar snap or snow pea pods
2 heads baby bok choy, leaves separated
4 ounces (113 g) shiitake mushrooms, sliced
1 medium onion, cut into 1-inch pieces
1 red bell pepper, cut into 1-inch pieces
2 garlic cloves, crushed and chopped
½ cup kimchi
2 tbsps. cooking oil
2 tbsps. gochujang
2 tbsps. soy sauce
1 tbsp. ginger, crushed and chopped

DIRECTIONS:

1. In a wok, heat the cooking oil over high heat until it shimmers.
2. Add the garlic, ginger, and onion and stir-fry for 1 minute.
3. Place the mushrooms and pea pods and stir-fry for 1 minute.
4. Toss the bell pepper and bok choy and stir-fry for 1 minute.
5. Pour the kimchi, gochujang and soy sauce and stir-fry for 1 minute.
6. Serve hot.

Japanese Stir-Fried Carrot and Bean Sprouts

Prep Time: 8 minutes, Cook Time: 5 minutes, Serves: 3

INGREDIENTS:

2 cups bean sprouts
1 medium carrot, roll-cut into ½-inch pieces
4 ounces (113 g) shiitake mushrooms, cut into slices
1 medium onion, cut into 1-inch pieces
1 red bell pepper, cut into 1-inch pieces
4 scallions, cut into 1-inch pieces
2 garlic cloves, crushed and chopped
2 tbsps. yellow miso
2 tbsps. mirin
2 tbsps. tamari
1 tbsp. toasted sesame oil
2 tbsps. cooking oil
1 tbsp. ginger, crushed and chopped

DIRECTIONS:

1. Whisk together the miso, mirin, tamari and sesame oil in a small bowl. Set aside.
2. In a wok, heat the cooking oil over high heat until it shimmers.
3. Add the ginger, garlic and carrot and stir-fry for 1 minute.
4. Place the onion and mushrooms and stir-fry for 1 minute.
5. Then put the bell pepper and scallions and stir-fry for 1 minute.
6. Pour the miso mixture and toss for 30 seconds.
7. Garnish with bean sprouts and serve.

Eggplant and Tofu in Garlic Sauce

Prep Time: 7 minutes, Cook Time: 25 minutes, Serves: 4

INGREDIENTS:

3 long Chinese eggplants (about ¾ pound / 340 g), trimmed and sliced diagonally into 1-inch pieces
½ pound (227 g) firm tofu, cut into ½-inch cubes
6 cups water plus 1 tbsp., divided
3 garlic cloves, chopped
3 tbsps. vegetable oil, divided
1½ tbsps. cornstarch, divided
1 tbsp. light soy sauce
1 tbsp. kosher salt
2 tsps. sugar
1 tsp. peeled minced fresh ginger
½ tsp. dark soy sauce

DIRECTIONS:

1. Combine the 6 cups of water and salt in a large bowl. Stir slightly to dissolve the salt and place the eggplant pieces. Put a large pot lid on top to keep the eggplant submerged in the water and let rest for about 15 minutes. Drain the eggplant and use paper towels to pat dry. Toss the eggplant in a bowl with a dusting of cornstarch, about 1 tbsp..
2. Stir the remaining ½ tbsp. cornstarch with the remaining 1 tbsp. of water, light soy, sugar and dark soy in a small bowl. Set aside.
3. Heat a wok over high heat until a drop of water sizzles and evaporates on contact. Add 2 tbsps. of oil and swirl to coat the base of the wok and up its sides. Place the eggplant in a single layer in the wok.
4. Sear the eggplant on each side, for about 4 minutes per side. The eggplant should be slightly charred and golden brown. If the wok begins to smoke, lower the heat to medium. Take the eggplant to a bowl and return the wok to the heat.
5. Pour the remaining 1 tbsp. of oil and stir-fry the garlic and ginger until they are fragrant and sizzling, about 10 seconds. Place the tofu and stir-fry for another 2 minutes, then return the eggplant to the wok. Stir the sauce again and pour into the wok, tossing all the ingredients together until the sauce thickens to a dark, glossy consistency.
6. Remove the eggplant and tofu to a platter and serve warm.

Traditional Cantonese Vegetables

Prep Time: 12 minutes, Cook Time: 6 minutes, Serves: 4

INGREDIENTS:

1 cup sliced mushrooms
1 cup 1-inch cut bok choy or Chinese cabbage
1 medium carrot, roll-cut into ½-inch pieces
1 medium onion, quartered and cut into 1-inch pieces
1 medium red bell pepper, cut into 1-inch pieces

4 scallions, cut diagonally into 1-inch slices
2 garlic cloves, crushed and chopped
¼ cup soy sauce
2 tbsps. cooking oil
1 tbsp. cornstarch
1 tbsp. brown sugar
1 tbsp. ginger, crushed and chopped

DIRECTIONS:

1. Whisk together the soy sauce, cornstarch, and brown sugar to form a roux in a small bowl. Set aside.
2. In a wok, heat the cooking oil over high heat until it shimmers.
3. Add the carrot, ginger, and garlic and stir-fry for 1 minute.
4. Then place the onion and mushrooms and stir-fry for 1 minute.
5. Put the bell pepper and stir-fry for 1 minute.
6. Add the bok choy and toss with the other ingredients.
7. Pour the roux and mix until a light glaze forms.
8. Toss in the scallions. Serve hot.

Vietnamese Vegetables with Rice Wine

Prep Time: 8 minutes, Cook Time: 4 minutes, Serves: 2

INGREDIENTS:

2 cups sugar snap or snow pea pods
1 cup sliced mushrooms
1 cup ¼-inch sliced Napa cabbage
½ cup coarsely chopped cilantro, parsley, dill, or mint
1 medium red onion, diced

3 scallions, minced
1 chile, cut crosswise, into ⅛- to ¼-inch rings
2 garlic cloves, crushed and chopped
2 tbsps. fish sauce
2 tbsps. rice wine
1 tbsp. cooking oil
¼ tsp. ground white pepper

DIRECTIONS:

1. In a wok, heat the cooking oil over high heat until it shimmers.
2. Place the scallions, onion and garlic and stir-fry for 30 seconds.
3. Toss the mushrooms and chile and stir-fry for 30 seconds.
4. Then put the pea pods and cabbage and stir-fry for 30 seconds.
5. Toss the fish sauce, rice wine and white pepper with the vegetables for 30 seconds.
6. Top with the fresh herbs of your choice and serve.

Chinese Ma Po Tofu

Prep Time: 10 minutes, Cook Time: 23 minutes, Serves: 6

INGREDIENTS:

1 pound (454 g) medium tofu, drained and cut into ½-inch cubes
½ pound (227 g) ground pork
1½ cups low-sodium chicken broth
4 scallions, thinly sliced, divided
3 tbsps. doubanjiang (Chinese chili bean paste)
2 tbsps. Shaoxing rice wine
1½ tbsps. water

2 tbsps. vegetable oil
1 tbsp. Sichuan peppercorns, crushed
1 tbsp. coarsely chopped fresh cilantro leaves, for garnish
2 tsps. light soy sauce
2 tsps. cornstarch
1 tsp. peeled finely minced fresh ginger
1 tsp. chili oil
1 tsp. sugar
½ tsp. Chinese five spice powder
Kosher salt

DIRECTIONS:

1. Mix together the ground pork, rice wine, light soy, and ginger in a small bowl. Set aside. Combine the cornstarch together with the water in another small bowl. Set aside.
2. Heat a wok over medium-high heat and add the vegetable oil. Place the Sichuan peppercorns and sauté slowly until they begin to sizzle as the oil heats up.
3. Put the marinated pork and bean paste and stir-fry for 4 to 5 minutes, until the pork is browned and crumbled. Add half the scallions, the chili oil, five spice powder and sugar. Continue to stir-fry for another 30 seconds, or until the scallions wilt.
4. Sprinkle the tofu cubes over the pork and pour in the broth. Do not stir; allow the tofu to cook and firm up a bit first. Cover and simmer for about 15 minutes over medium heat. Remove the lid and stir gently. Be careful not to break up the tofu cubes too much.
5. Taste and season with salt or sugar, depending on your preference. Additional sugar can calm down the spiciness if it's too hot. Toss the cornstarch and water again and pour to the tofu. Slowly toss until the sauce thickens.
6. Top with the remaining scallions and cilantro and serve warm.

Hunan-Style Tofu with Doubanjiang

Prep Time: 8 minutes, Cook Time: 8 minutes, Serves: 4

INGREDIENTS:

1 pound (454 g) firm tofu, drained and cut into ½-inch-thick squares, 2 inches across
1 large red bell pepper, cut into 1-inch pieces
4 scallions, cut into 2-inch sections
¼ cup low-sodium chicken or vegetable broth
3 garlic cloves, finely minced
1-inch piece fresh ginger, peeled and finely minced
4 tbsps. vegetable or canola oil, divided
3 tbsps. fermented black beans, rinsed and smashed
2 tbsps. doubanjiang (Chinese chili bean paste)
1 tbsp. water
1 tbsp. Shaoxing rice wine
1 tsp. cornstarch
1 tsp. sugar
Kosher salt

DIRECTIONS:

1. Stir together the cornstarch and water in a small bowl and set aside.
2. Heat a wok over high heat until a drop of water sizzles and evaporates on contact. Add 2 tbsps. of oil and swirl to coat the base and sides of the wok well. Season with a pinch of salt and place the tofu slices in the wok in one layer. Sear the tofu for 1 to 2 minutes, tilting the wok around to slip the oil under the tofu while it sears. When the first side is browned, carefully flip the tofu with a wok spatula and sear for another 1 to 2 minutes until golden brown. Transfer the seared tofu to a serving plate and set aside.
3. Lower the heat to medium-low. Pour the remaining 2 tbsps. of oil to the wok. Once the oil begins to slightly smoke, add the bean paste, black beans, ginger, and garlic. Stir-fry for about 20 seconds, or until the oil takes on a deep red color from the bean paste.
4. Place the bell pepper and scallions and toss with the Shaoxing wine and sugar. Cook for another minute, or until the wine is nearly evaporated and the bell pepper is soft.
5. Lightly fold in the fried tofu until all the ingredients in the wok are mixed. Continue to cook for 45 seconds more, or until the tofu appears a deep red color and the scallions have wilted.
6. Pour the chicken broth over the tofu mixture and gently toss to deglaze the wok and dissolve any of the stuck bits on the wok. Give the cornstarch-water mixture a quick stir and add to the wok. Slowly stir and simmer for 2 minutes, or until the sauce is glossy and thick. Serve warm.

Garlic Eggs and Bok Choy

Prep Time: 5 minutes, Cook Time: 5 minutes, Serves: 3

INGREDIENTS:

6 eggs, beaten
1 cup chopped bok choy
3 scallions, cut into ½-inch pieces
3 garlic cloves, crushed and chopped
¼ cup hoisin sauce
2 tbsps. cooking oil
2 tbsps. soy sauce
2 tbsps. rice wine

DIRECTIONS:

1. In a wok, heat the cooking oil over high heat until it shimmers.
2. Put the garlic and stir-fry for 10 to 15 seconds or until lightly browned.
3. Pour the eggs and rice wine and stir-fry until the eggs are firm but still moist.
4. Place the scallions and stir-fry for 30 seconds.
5. Then add the bok choy and stir-fry for 1 minute.
6. Combine the soy sauce and hoisin sauce in a small bowl. Drizzle over the scrambled eggs. Serve warm.

Tasty Curried Tofu

Prep Time: 8 minutes, Cook Time: 6 minutes, Serves: 6

INGREDIENTS:

1 pound (454 g) extra-firm tofu, well drained, patted dry, and cut into 1-inch pieces
4 ounces (113 g) mushrooms, cut into slices
1 medium carrot, roll-cut into ½-inch pieces
1 medium onion, cut into 1-inch pieces
1 red bell pepper, cut into 1-inch pieces
2 garlic cloves, crushed and chopped
½ cup vegetable or meat broth
2 tbsps. curry of choice
2 tbsps. cooking oil
2 tbsps. rice vinegar
2 tbsps. cornstarch
2 tbsps. soy sauce
1 tbsp. ginger, crushed and chopped

DIRECTIONS:

1. Whisk together the curry, rice vinegar, soy sauce, broth and cornstarch in a small bowl. Set aside.
2. In a wok, heat the cooking oil over high heat until it shimmers.
3. Add the ginger, garlic, and tofu and stir-fry for 2 minutes, or until the tofu begins to brown.
4. Put the carrot and onion and stir-fry for 1 minute.
5. Then place the mushrooms and bell pepper and stir-fry for 1 minute.
6. Pour the curry mixture to the wok and stir-fry until a glaze forms.
7. Serve hot.

Malaysian Curried Vegetables

Prep Time: 5 minutes, Cook Time: 6 minutes, Serves: 2

INGREDIENTS:

2 cups sugar snap or snow pea pods	1 tbsp. ginger, crushed and chopped
1 medium carrot, roll-cut into ½-inch pieces	1 tbsp. hot sesame oil
1 medium red onion, diced	1 tsp. Chinese five-spice powder
¼ cup unsweetened and shredded dried coconut	½ tsp. ground chili powder
2 tbsps. soy sauce	¼ tsp. ground fennel
2 tbsps. coconut oil	¼ tsp. ground cumin

DIRECTIONS:

1. Whisk together the soy sauce, sesame oil, five-spice powder, cumin, fennel and chili powder in a small bowl. Set aside.
2. In a wok, heat the coconut oil over high heat until it shimmers.
3. Place the ginger and carrot and stir-fry for 1 minute.
4. Add the onion and stir-fry for 1 minute.
5. Then toss the pea pods and the soy sauce mixture and stir-fry for 1 minute.
6. Put the coconut and stir-fry for 1 minute.
7. Serve warm.

Sesame Asparagus with Soy Sauce

Prep Time: 5 minutes, Cook Time: 8 minutes, Serves: 4

INGREDIENTS:

2 pounds (907 g) asparagus, trimmed and cut diagonally into 2-inch-long pieces	2 tbsps. light soy sauce
	1 tbsp. toasted sesame seeds
	1 tbsp. vegetable oil
2 large garlic cloves, coarsely chopped	1 tsp. sugar
2 tbsps. sesame oil	Kosher salt

DIRECTIONS:

1. Stir the light soy and sugar together in a small bowl, until the sugar dissolves. Set aside.
2. Heat a wok over high heat until a drop of water sizzles and evaporates on contact. Add the vegetable oil and swirl to coat the base of the wok well. Place the garlic and stir-fry until fragrant, about 10 seconds.
3. Put the asparagus and stir-fry until crisp-tender, about 4 minutes, seasoning with a small pinch of salt when stir-frying. Pour the soy sauce mixture and stir to coat the asparagus, cooking for about 1 minute more.

4. Pour the sesame oil over the asparagus and transfer to a plate. Garnish with the sesame seeds and serve warm.

Stir-Fried Spicy Napa Cabbage

Prep Time: 6 minutes, Cook Time: 7 minutes, Serves: 4

INGREDIENTS:

1 head napa cabbage, shredded	2 tbsps. vegetable oil
3 or 4 dried chili peppers	1 tbsp. light soy sauce
2 peeled fresh ginger slices, each about the size of a quarter	½ tbsp. black vinegar
	Kosher salt
	Freshly ground black pepper
2 garlic cloves, sliced	

DIRECTIONS:

1. Heat a wok over medium-high heat until a drop of water sizzles and evaporates on contact. Add the oil and swirl to coat the base of the wok well. Season the oil with the chilies. Let the chilies sizzle in the oil for 15 seconds. Place the ginger slices and a pinch of salt. Let the ginger sizzle in the oil for about 30 seconds, swirling slowly. Toss the garlic in and stir-fry lightly to flavor the oil, about 10 seconds. Do not let the garlic turn brown or burn.
2. Place the cabbage and stir-fry until it wilts and turns bright green, about 4 minutes. Pour the light soy and black vinegar and season with a pinch of salt and pepper. Toss to coat for another 20 to 30 seconds.
3. Remove to a platter and discard the ginger. Serve warm.

Stir-Fried Vegetables with Oyster Sauce

Prep Time: 7 minutes, Cook Time: 5 minutes, Serves: 2 to 4

INGREDIENTS:

2 cups sugar snap or snow pea pods	1-inch pieces
	¼ cup oyster sauce
12 cherry tomatoes, cut in half	2 garlic cloves, crushed and chopped
1 medium carrot, roll-cut into ½-inch pieces	2 tbsps. soy sauce
1 medium onion, diced	2 tbsps. cooking oil
1 red bell pepper, cut into	1 tbsp. ginger, crushed and chopped

DIRECTIONS:

1. In a wok, heat the cooking oil over high heat until it shimmers.

2. Add the garlic, ginger and carrot and stir-fry for 1 minute.
3. Place the onion and stir-fry for 1 minute.
4. Then put the cherry tomatoes and stir-fry for 1 minute.
5. Toss the pea pods and bell pepper and stir-fry for 1 minute.
6. Pour the oyster sauce and soy sauce and stir until a light glaze forms.
7. Serve hot.

Quick Chinese Broccoli with Oyster Sauce

Prep Time: 4 minutes, Cook Time: 5 minutes, Serves: 2

INGREDIENTS:

2 bunches Chinese broccoli or broccolini, tough ends trimmed
¼ cup oyster sauce
4 peeled fresh ginger slices, each about the size of a quarter

4 garlic cloves, peeled
2 tbsps. vegetable oil
2 tbsps. water
2 tsps. light soy sauce
1 tsp. sesame oil
Kosher salt

DIRECTIONS:

1. Stir together the oyster sauce, light soy, and sesame oil in a small bowl, and set aside.
2. Heat a wok over high heat until a drop of water sizzles and evaporates on contact. Add the vegetable oil and swirl to coat the base of the wok well. Place the ginger, garlic and a pinch of salt. Let the aromatics sizzle in the oil, swirling slowly for about 10 seconds.
3. Put the broccoli and stir, tossing until coated with oil and bright green. Pour in the water and cover to steam the broccoli for 3 minutes, or until the stalks can easily be pierced with a knife. Remove the ginger and garlic and discard.
4. Mix in the sauce and toss to coat until hot. Take to a serving plate and serve warm.

Stir-Fried Savory Lettuce with Oyster Sauce

Prep Time: 5 minutes, Cook Time: 8 minutes, Serves: 4 to 6

INGREDIENTS:

1 head iceberg lettuce, rinsed and spun dry, cut into 1-inch-wide pieces
1 peeled fresh ginger

slice, about the size of a quarter
2 garlic cloves, thinly sliced

2 tbsps. oyster sauce
1½ tbsps. vegetable oil
½ tsp. sesame oil, for

garnish
Kosher salt

DIRECTIONS:

1. Heat a wok over high heat until a drop of water sizzles and evaporates on contact. Pour the vegetable oil and swirl to coat the base of the wok well. Season the oil with the ginger slice and a pinch of salt. Let the ginger sizzle in the oil for about 30 seconds, swirling slowly.
2. Place the garlic and stir-fry lightly to flavor the oil, about 10 seconds. Do not let the garlic turn brown or burn. Put the lettuce and stir-fry until it begins to wilt slightly, 3 to 4 minutes. Pour the oyster sauce over the lettuce and quickly toss to coat, another 20 to 30 seconds.
3. Transfer the lettuce to a platter, discard the ginger, and drizzle with the sesame oil. Serve warm.

Stir-Fried Bok Choy and Shiitake Mushrooms

Prep Time: 8 minutes, Cook Time: 10 minutes, Serves: 6

INGREDIENTS:

1½ pounds (680 g) baby bok choy, sliced crosswise into 1-inch pieces
½ pound (227 g) fresh shiitake mushrooms, stems removed and caps cut into quarters
1 peeled fresh ginger

slice, about the size of a quarter
2 garlic cloves, minced
3 tbsps. vegetable oil
2 tbsps. Shaoxing rice wine
2 tsps. sesame oil
2 tsps. light soy sauce
Kosher salt

DIRECTIONS:

1. Heat a wok over high heat until a drop of water sizzles and evaporates on contact. Add the vegetable oil and swirl to coat the base of the wok well. Season the oil with the ginger slice and a pinch of salt. Let the ginger sizzle in the oil for about 30 seconds, swirling slowly.
2. Place the mushrooms and stir-fry for 3 to 4 minutes, until they just begin to brown. Put the garlic and stir-fry until fragrant, about 30 seconds more.
3. Add the bok choy and stir with the mushrooms. The wok may appear crowded, but the bok choy will wilt down immediately. Pour the rice wine, light soy and sesame oil. Cook for 3 to 4 minutes, tossing the vegetables frequently until they are soft.
4. Take the vegetables to a serving platter and discard the ginger. Serve hot.

Stir-Fried Sweet Snow Peas

Prep Time: 5 minutes, Cook Time: 5 minutes, Serves: 4

INGREDIENTS:

¾ pound (340 g) snow peas or sugar snap peas, strings removed
2 peeled fresh ginger

slices, each about the size of a quarter
2 tbsps. vegetable oil
Kosher salt

DIRECTIONS:

1. Heat a wok over high heat until a drop of water sizzles and evaporates on contact. Add the oil and swirl to coat the base of the wok well. Season the oil with ginger slices and a pinch of salt. Let the ginger sizzle in the oil for about 30 seconds, swirling slowly.
2. Place the snow peas and, using a wok spatula, toss to coat with oil. Stir-fry for about 2 to 3 minutes, until become bright green and crisp tender.
3. Take the snow peas to a platter and discard the ginger. Serve warm.

Stir-Fried Garlic Spinach with Soy Sauce

Prep Time: 2 minutes, Cook Time: 4 minutes, Serves: 2

INGREDIENTS:

8 ounces (227 g) prewashed baby spinach
4 garlic cloves, thinly sliced

2 tbsps. vegetable oil
1 tbsp. light soy sauce
1 tsp. sugar
Kosher salt

DIRECTIONS:

1. Stir together the light soy and sugar in a small bowl, until the sugar is dissolved and set aside.
2. Heat a wok over high heat until a drop of water sizzles and evaporates on contact. Add the oil and swirl to coat the base of the wok well. Place the garlic and a pinch of salt and stir-fry, tossing until the garlic is tender, about 10 seconds. Remove the garlic from the pan with a slotted spoon, and set aside.
3. Put the spinach to the seasoned oil and stir-fry until the greens are just wilted and bright green. Pour the sugar and soy mixture and toss to coat well. Take the garlic back to the wok and toss to incorporate. Transfer to a serving dish and serve warm.

Classic Indian Five-Spice Vegetables

Prep Time: 10 minutes, Cook Time: 6 minutes, Serves: 3

INGREDIENTS:

2 cups sugar snap pea pods
1 medium carrot, roll-cut into ½-inch pieces
1 medium onion, cut into 1-inch pieces
1 medium poblano pepper, cut into 1-inch pieces
1 red bell pepper, cut into 1-inch pieces

4 scallions, cut into 1-inch slices
2 garlic cloves, crushed and chopped
2 tbsps. cooking oil
¼ tsp. ground cloves
¼ tsp. ground turmeric
¼ tsp. ground cumin
¼ tsp. ground coriander
¼ tsp. ground fennel
1 tsp. hot sesame oil

DIRECTIONS:

1. In a wok, heat the cooking oil over high heat until it shimmers.
2. Place the garlic and carrot and stir-fry for 1 minute.
3. Put the onion and stir-fry for 1 minute.
4. Then add the pea pods and stir-fry for 1 minute.
5. Place the poblano and bell peppers and stir-fry for 1 minute.
6. Toss the scallions, cumin, coriander, turmeric, cloves, fennel and sesame oil and stir-fry for 30 seconds.
7. Serve hot.

String Beans with Pork, page 19

Asian Yellow Peas with Spinach, page 18

Mexican Wok Black Beans and Zucchinis, page 20

Quinoa Fried Rice with Beans, page 18

Chapter 4: Beans and Legumes

Quinoa Fried Rice with Beans

Prep Time: 10 minutes, Cook Time: 5 minutes, Serves: 4 to 6

INGREDIENTS:

6 cups cooked quinoa
1 cup frozen peas and carrots (no need to thaw)
3 or 4 string beans, cut into ¼-inch pieces
2 eggs, lightly beaten
3 garlic cloves, minced
1 scallion, chopped
2 tbsps. peanut oil
2 tbsps. soy sauce

DIRECTIONS:

1. In a wok, heat the peanut oil over medium-high heat.
2. In the wok, scramble the eggs until cooked, then take them to a small bowl.
3. Place the garlic to the wok and stir-fry for 20 seconds. Put the string beans and stir-fry for about 20 to 30 seconds.
4. Pour in more peanut oil if necessary, then arrange the peas and carrots and stir-fry for 30 seconds.
5. Place the quinoa and return the scrambled egg to the wok, stirring to combine well.
6. Toss in the soy sauce. Stir-fry gently to combine with a wok spatula.
7. Transfer to a serving dish and top with the chopped scallion.

Chili Dry-Fried String Beans

Prep Time: 5 minutes, Cook Time: 7 minutes, Serves: 4 to 6

INGREDIENTS:

SAUCE:
1 tbsp. Shaoxing wine
1 tsp. sesame oil
1 tsp. sugar
1 tsp. chili bean sauce
½ tsp. salt
STRING BEANS:
1 pound (454 g) fresh string beans, trimmed
8 dried red chile peppers
3 garlic cloves, minced
½-inch piece ginger, peeled and julienned
1 tbsp. peanut oil

DIRECTIONS:

1. Prepare the sauce by mixing together the Shaoxing wine, chili bean sauce, sesame oil, sugar and salt in a small bowl. Set it aside.
2. In a wok, heat the peanut oil over medium-high heat.
3. When the wok starts to smoke, add the green beans. Stir-fry until they are blistered and bright green, for 5 minutes. If the beans start to burn, reduce the heat to medium.
4. Place the ginger, dried red chiles and garlic to the wok. Fry until fragrant, then pour in the sauce. Stir to mix all the ingredients.
5. Transfer to a plate and serve warm.

Asian Yellow Peas with Spinach

Prep Time: 10 minutes, Cook Time: 40 minutes, Serves: 5

INGREDIENTS:

2 cups yellow split peas
8 ounces (227 g) spinach, washed and coarsely chopped
1 medium chili serrano, stemmed and thinly chopped
5 big garlic cloves, peeled and finely minced
¼ cup fresh ginger,
peeled and finely chopped
8 cups water
8 tsps. butter unsalted
2 tsps. freshly squeezed lemon juice
2 tsps. cumin seeds
1½ tsps. turmeric
2 tsps. salt, plus more as required

DIRECTIONS:

1. In a fine-mesh strainer, arrange the split peas and rinse them vigorously under cold water. Transfer to a wide saucepan, pour in the water you have weighed, and bring to a boil over high heat.
2. Reduce the heat to medium-low and simmer for about 30 minutes, using a large spoon to stir and skim any scum off the surface until the peas are completely soft and the consistency of split pea soup thickens.
3. Set aside, remove from the heat, and place the lemon juice and the measured salt in it.
4. In a wok over medium heat, heat the butter until it is foamed. Place the cumin seeds and turmeric in it and simmer for around 3 minutes, until the cumin seeds are toasted and fragrant and the butter is very foamy, stirring periodically.
5. Put the garlic, ginger and serrano and season with salt. Simmer for 2 to 3 minutes, stirring occasionally, until the vegetables are soft. Place the spinach and simmer until the spinach is entirely wilted, stirring occasionally, for around 4 minutes.
6. Transfer the spinach mixture to the reserved saucepan with the split peas, and mix to blend. Serve warm.

String Beans with Pork

Prep Time: 35 minutes, Cook Time: 5 minutes, Serves: 6 to 8

INGREDIENTS:

1 pound (454 g) green beans, trimmed and cut into 1-inch pieces	1 tbsp. oyster sauce
	2 tsps. soy sauce
	2 tsps. Shaoxing wine
¼ pound (113 g) ground pork	1 tsp. sugar
	Pinch salt
2 garlic cloves, minced	Pinch ground white pepper
1 tbsp. peanut oil	

DIRECTIONS:

1. Mix together the oyster sauce, Shaoxing wine, soy sauce, sugar, pepper and salt in a small bowl. Add the mixture over the ground pork, mix to combine well, and marinate for about 20 minutes.
2. In a wok, heat the peanut oil over medium-high heat.
3. Place the ground pork and stir-fry for about 1 minute, or until partially cooked. Put the green beans and garlic.
4. Reduce the heat to low, and continue to cook until the green beans are soft, for 2 to 3 minutes, pouring water to the wok to help steam the green beans if needed.
5. Transfer to a plate and serve.

Stir-Fried String Beans

Prep Time: 8 minutes, Cook Time: 5 minutes, Serves: 4

INGREDIENTS:

1 pound (454 g) green beans, trimmed, cut in half, and blotted dry	1 tbsp. doubanjiang (Chinese chili bean paste)
½ cup vegetable oil	2 tsps. sugar
1 tbsp. minced garlic	1 tsp. sesame oil
1 tbsp. light soy sauce	Kosher salt

DIRECTIONS:

1. Stir together the light soy, garlic, bean paste, sugar, sesame oil and a pinch of salt in a small bowl. Set aside.
2. In a wok, heat the vegetable oil over medium-high heat to 375ºF (190ºC), or until it bubbles and sizzles around the end of a wooden spoon. Fry the green beans in batches of a couple handfuls at a time (the beans should just cover the oil in a single layer). Slowly turn the beans in the oil until they turn wrinkled, 45 seconds to 1 minute, then take the green beans to a paper towel–lined plate to drain.
3. When all the beans have been cooked, transfer the remaining oil to a heatproof container carefully.

Wipe and clean out the wok by a pair of tongs with a couple of paper towels.

4. Increase the wok to high heat and add 1 tbsp. of the reserved frying oil. Place the green beans and chili sauce, stir-frying until the sauce comes to a boil and coats the green beans well. Take the beans to a platter and serve warm.

Noodles with Green Beans and Cabbage

Prep Time: 15 minutes, Cook Time: 12 minutes, Serves: 6

INGREDIENTS:

½ pound (227 g) dried sweet potato noodles or mung bean noodles	2 peeled fresh ginger slices, each about the size of a quarter
½ pound (227 g) green beans, trimmed and halved	2 tbsps. vegetable oil
	2 tbsps. light soy sauce
	1 tbsp. oyster sauce
1 small head napa cabbage, chopped into bite-size pieces	2 tsps. dark soy sauce
	1 tsp. sugar
	Kosher salt
3 scallions, coarsely chopped	1 tsp. Sichuan peppercorns

DIRECTIONS:

1. In a large bowl, soak the noodles in hot water for 10 minutes to soften them. Gently drain the noodles in a colander. Rinse with cold water and let rest.
2. Mix together the light soy, dark soy, oyster sauce and sugar in a small bowl. Set aside.
3. Heat a wok over high heat until a drop of water sizzles and evaporates on contact. Add the oil and swirl to coat the base of the wok well. Season the oil with the ginger, a small pinch of salt and the Sichuan peppercorns. Let the ginger sizzle in the oil for about 30 seconds, swirling slowly. Remove the ginger and peppercorns and discard.
4. Place the napa cabbage and green beans to the wok and stir-fry, tossing and flipping for about 3 to 4 minutes, until the vegetables wilt. Stir in the sauce and toss to combine well.
5. Put the noodles and toss to combine with the sauce and vegetables. Cover the lid and lower the heat to medium. Cook for about 2 to 3 minutes, or until the noodles become transparent and the green beans are tender.
6. Increase the heat to medium-high and uncover the wok. Stir-fry, tossing and scooping for extra 1 to 2 minutes, until the sauce thickens slightly. Remove from the heat and garnish with the scallions. Serve warm.

Venetian Garlic Beans

Prep Time: 5 minutes, Cook Time: 11 minutes, Serves: 5

INGREDIENTS:

2 (15-ounce / 425-g) cans cut green beans, drained
¼ cup Italian style bread crumbs
2 to 3 cloves garlic, pressed
2 tbsps. butter

DIRECTIONS:

1. In a wok over medium heat, heat the butter.
2. Cook the beans and garlic for about 11 minutes. Stir in the bread crumbs and turn off the heat.
3. Season as your taste and serve it warm.

Saucy Green Beans Skillet

Prep Time: 5 minutes, Cook Time: 15 minutes, Serves: 4

INGREDIENTS:

14 ounces (397 g) green beans, trimmed and halved
1 tomato, diced
1 tbsp. olive oil
1 tsp. chopped garlic
Salt and pepper

DIRECTIONS:

1. Place a saucepan of salted water over medium heat and bring it to a boil.
2. Cook the beans for 9 minutes then drain them.
3. In a wok, heat the oil over medium heat. Cook the garlic for 35 seconds.
4. Add the beans and cook for about 2 to 3 minutes.
5. Stir in the tomato with a pinch of salt and pepper. Cook them for about 4 minutes.
6. Serve warm.

Mexican Wok Black Beans and Zucchinis

Prep Time: 14 minutes, Cook Time: 12 minutes, Serves: 6

INGREDIENTS:

1 (15-ounce / 425-g) can black beans, rinsed and drained
4 small zucchinis, diced
1 cup frozen whole kernel corn
1 large onion, chopped
1 fresh poblano chili pepper, seeded and chopped
3 cloves garlic, minced
1 tbsp. olive oil
½ tsp. salt

DIRECTIONS:

1. In a large wok on medium-high heat, heat the oil and

cook the onion and garlic until soft.
2. Place the zucchinis and poblano pepper and cook till tender.
3. Stir in the corn and black beans and cook till heated entirely.
4. Season with the salt to taste and serve warm.

Authentic Beans Caprese

Prep Time: 10 minutes, Cook Time: 15 minutes, Serves: 6

INGREDIENTS:

1½ pounds (680 g) green beans
½ pint cherry tomatoes, halved
1 tbsp. butter
1 tbsp. sugar
½ tsp. basil
¾ tsp. garlic salt
Salt and pepper

DIRECTIONS:

1. Put a large saucepan of water over high heat. Heat it until it starts boiling.
2. Add the green beans and cook for 7 minutes until they become tender. Drain them.
3. In a large wok over medium heat, heat the butter until it melts.
4. Place the garlic salt, sugar, basil, salt and pepper with cherry tomatoes and cook for 3 minutes.
5. Toss in the green beans and cook them for another 2 minutes.
6. Serve hot.

Curry Garbanzo with Tomato

Prep Time: 10 minutes, Cook Time: 20 minutes, Serves: 6

INGREDIENTS:

1 (16-ounce / 454-g) cans garbanzo beans
½ cup tomatoes, diced
1 onion, diced
Coriander leaves
1 tbsp. ghee
1 tsp. coriander powder
1 tsp. garam masala
1 tsp. chili powder
1 tsp. ginger, grated
1 tsp. garlic, minced
1 tsp. cumin powder
1 tsp. turmeric
Lemon slices for serving

DIRECTIONS:

1. In a wok, heat the ghee over medium heat.
2. Add garlic, onion and ginger and cook for 6 minutes.
3. Toss in the tomatoes, cumin, coriander, turmeric, chili powder and salt.
4. Cook for about 6 minutes. Stir in the garbanzo beans and cook them for about 3 minutes.
5. Put the garam masala and cook for about 2 minutes.
6. Season as your taste. Serve it hot with some lemon slices.

Green Bean with Chicken Thighs

Prep Time: 15 minutes, Cook Time: 10 minutes, Serves: 6

INGREDIENTS:

¾ pound (340 g) green beans, trimmed and halved crosswise diagonally
¾ pound (340 g) boneless, skinless chicken thighs, sliced across the grain into bite-size strips
¼ cup slivered almonds, toasted
4 peeled fresh ginger slices, each about the size of a quarter
3 tbsps. Shaoxing rice wine, divided
3 tbsps. vegetable oil, divided
2 tbsps. light soy sauce
1 tbsp. seasoned rice vinegar
2 tsps. sesame oil
2 tsps. cornstarch
Kosher salt
Red pepper flakes

DIRECTIONS:

1. Combine the chicken with 1 tbsp. of rice wine, cornstarch, a small pinch of salt, and a pinch of red pepper flakes in a mixing bowl. Stir to coat the chicken evenly. Marinate for about 10 minutes.
2. Heat a wok over high heat until a drop of water sizzles and evaporates on contact. Add 2 tbsps. of vegetable oil and swirl to coat the base of the wok well. Season the oil with the ginger and a small pinch of salt. Let the ginger sizzle in the oil for 30 seconds, swirling slowly.
3. Place the chicken and marinade to the wok and stir-fry for about 3 to 4 minutes, or until the chicken is slightly seared and no longer pink. Take to a clean bowl and set aside.
4. Pour in the remaining 1 tbsp. of vegetable oil and stir-fry the green beans for 2 to 3 minutes, or until they become bright green. Take the chicken back to the wok and toss together. Add the remaining 2 tbsps. of rice wine, vinegar and light soy. Toss to combine and coat well. Let the green beans simmer for 3 more minutes, or until the green beans are soft. Remove the ginger and throw away.
5. Sprinkle with the almonds and transfer to a platter. Drizzle with the sesame oil and serve warm.

Caramelized Balsamic Bean with Onion

Prep Time: 5 minutes, Cook Time: 16 minutes, Serves: 4

INGREDIENTS:

1 pound (454 g) green beans, trimmed and halved
1 medium red onion wedges
1 cup water
2 tbsps. olive oil
2 tsps. balsamic vinegar
1 tsp. salt
¼ tsp. ground pepper

DIRECTIONS:

1. In a wok over medium heat, heat the oil. Add 1 cup water, salt and pepper until they start simmering.
2. Toss in onion with green beans. Cover the lid and cook for about 9 minutes.
3. Once the time is up, uncover the lid. Cook for another 7 minutes.
4. Pour in vinegar and stir to coat well. Serve warm.

Five-Spice Lamb and Green Beans

Prep Time: 10 minutes, Cook Time: 4 minutes, Serves: 4

INGREDIENTS:

1 pound (454 g) ground lamb
2 cups fresh green beans
1 medium onion, diced
2 garlic cloves, crushed and chopped
1 tbsp. ginger, crushed
and chopped
¼ cup oyster sauce
2 tbsps. cooking oil
1 tbsp. Chinese five-spice powder
1 tsp. hot sesame oil

DIRECTIONS:

1. In a wok, heat the cooking oil over high heat until it shimmers.
2. Place the garlic, ginger, lamb and onion and stir-fry for about 1 minute.
3. Put the green beans, five-spice powder, and sesame oil and stir-fry for 1 minute.
4. Add the oyster sauce and stir-fry for about 1 minute.
5. Serve warm.

Indonesian Tomato Egg Fried Rice, page 24

Japanese Fried Rice with Bacon, page 25

Shrimp Fried Rice with Peas, page 23

Vegetable Egg Fried Rice, page 25

Chapter 5: Grain and Rice

Shrimp Fried Rice with Peas

Prep Time: 15 minutes, Cook Time: 4 minutes, Serves: 6

INGREDIENTS:

2 cups cold, cooked rice
½ pound (227 g) medium shrimp, peeled, deveined, and halved lengthwise
1 cup frozen peas, thawed
2 large eggs, beaten
1 medium onion, diced
4 scallions, cut into ½-inch pieces
2 garlic cloves, crushed and chopped
2 tbsps. cooking oil
1 tbsp. ginger, crushed and chopped
1 tbsp. soy sauce
1 tsp. sesame oil
½ tsp. kosher salt

DIRECTIONS:

1. In a wok, heat the cooking oil over high heat until it shimmers.
2. Add the garlic, ginger, salt and eggs and stir-fry for about 1 minute, or until the eggs are firm.
3. Place the onion and shrimp and stir-fry for about 1 minute.
4. Toss the peas, sesame oil, rice and soy sauce and stir-fry for 1 minute.
5. Sprinkle with the scallions and serve hot.

Kimchi Fried Rice with Mushroom

Prep Time: 12 minutes, Cook Time: 6 minutes, Serves: 4

INGREDIENTS:

½ pound (227 g) thick-sliced bacon, cut into 1-inch pieces
2 cups cold, cooked rice
1 cup kimchi, cut into ½-inch pieces
4 ounces (113 g) sliced mushrooms
4 large eggs
4 scallions, cut into ½-inch pieces
2 garlic cloves, crushed and chopped
¼ cup kimchi juice
1 tbsp. ginger, crushed and chopped
1 tbsp. soy sauce
1 tsp. sesame oil

DIRECTIONS:

1. In a wok over high heat, place the bacon, ginger and garlic and stir-fry for 2 minutes, or until the bacon is lightly browned.
2. Drain off all but 2 tbsps. of the bacon fat from the wok and let rest.
3. Add the mushrooms to the wok and stir-fry for about 1 minute.
4. Place the kimchi and stir-fry for 30 seconds.
5. Toss in the rice, sesame oil, soy sauce, scallions and kimchi juice. Stir-fry for about 30 seconds, then transfer to a serving dish.
6. Take 2 tbsps. of the reserved bacon fat back to the wok and fry the eggs sunny-side up.
7. Top the fried eggs over the rice and serve.

Traditional Yangzhou Fried Rice

Prep Time: 8 minutes, Cook Time: 8 minutes, Serves: 4 to 6

INGREDIENTS:

6 cups cooked white or brown rice (about 2 cups uncooked)
½ pound (227 g) shrimp, peeled and deveined
2 eggs, lightly beaten
½ cup diced ham
½ cup frozen peas (no need to thaw)
1 small onion, diced
3 scallions, finely chopped
2 tbsps. peanut oil (divided), plus more as needed
2 tsps. soy sauce
1 tsp. salt
2 pinches ground white pepper

DIRECTIONS:

1. In a wok, heat 1 tbsp. of peanut oil over medium-high heat.
2. Add the eggs into the wok, cook until firm, and break the egg into small pieces with a wok spatula. Take the egg from the wok and set it aside.
3. Drizzle a little more peanut oil to the wok if needed, place the shrimp and stir-fry until fully cooked. Remove and set aside with the egg.
4. Pour in the remaining 1 tbsp. of oil to the wok, and swirl to coat the bottom surface with the wok spatula.
5. Place the onion and diced ham and stir-fry until the onion turns slightly translucent.
6. Put the frozen peas and stir-fry for a few seconds.
7. Toss in the cooked rice, sprinkle with the salt and pepper and add the soy sauce. Stir-fry for 1 minute to season and heat the rice.
8. Take the scrambled egg and shrimp back to the wok, and sprinkle the chopped scallions, stirring to combine all the ingredients well.
9. Serve hot.

Indonesian Tomato Egg Fried Rice

Prep Time: 6 minutes, Cook Time: 5 minutes, Serves: 4

INGREDIENTS:

2 cups cold, cooked rice
4 eggs
2 tomatoes, sliced
½ pound (227 g) ground meat of your choice
1 cucumber, sliced
1 medium onion, diced
4 scallions, cut into ½-inch pieces
2 garlic cloves, crushed and chopped
¼ cup kecap manis
3 tbsps. cooking oil, divided
1 tbsp. ginger, crushed and chopped
1 tsp. hot sesame oil

DIRECTIONS:

1. In a wok, heat 2 tbsps. of the cooking oil over high heat until it shimmers.
2. Add the meat, garlic, ginger and onion and stir-fry for about 1 minute.
3. Place the rice, sesame oil, kecap manis and scallions and stir-fry for 1 minute. Transfer to a serving bowl.
4. Pour the remaining 1 tbsp. of cooking oil to the wok and, once the oil is shimmering, fry the eggs sunny-side up.
5. Put a fried egg on top of rice, and sliced tomatoes and cucumbers on the side. Serve warm.

Fried Rice with Shrimp and Egg

Prep Time: 10 minutes, Cook Time: 10 minutes, Serves: 4

INGREDIENTS:

1 large egg, beaten
½ pound (227 g) shrimp (any size), peeled, deveined, and cut into bite-size pieces
2 garlic cloves, finely minced
½ cup frozen peas and carrots
2 scallions, thinly sliced,
divided
3 cups cold cooked rice
3 tbsps. unsalted butter
2 tbsps. vegetable oil
1 tbsp. light soy sauce
1 tbsp. sesame oil
1 tsp. peeled finely minced fresh ginger
Kosher salt

DIRECTIONS:

1. Heat a wok over high heat until a drop of water sizzles and evaporates on contact. Add the vegetable oil and swirl to coat the base of the wok well. Season the oil with a small pinch of salt. Place the egg and scramble quickly.
2. Push the egg to the sides of the wok to create a center ring, then put the shrimp, ginger and garlic together. Stir-fry the shrimp with a small pinch of salt for about 2 to 3 minutes, until they turn opaque and pink. Place the peas and carrots and half the scallions

and stir-fry for 1 more minute.
3. Add the rice, breaking up any large lumps, and sitr and flip to combine all of the ingredients. Stir-fry for about 1 minute, then push it all to the sides of the wok, creating a well in the bottom of the wok.
4. Pour in the butter and light soy, allow the butter to melt and bubble, then toss everything together to coat well, about 30 seconds.
5. Arrange the fried rice evenly in the wok and let the rice sit against the wok for about 2 minutes to crisp up slightly. Drizzle with sesame oil and season with a small pinch of salt. Remove from the heat and serve hot, garnishing with the rest of the scallions.

Fried Rice with Smoked Trout

Prep Time: 8 minutes, Cook Time: 10 minutes, Serves: 4

INGREDIENTS:

3 cups cold cooked rice
4 ounces (113 g) smoked trout, broken into bite-size pieces
2 large eggs
½ cup thinly sliced hearts of romaine lettuce
2 scallions, thinly sliced
2 garlic cloves, finely minced
3 tbsps. ghee or
vegetable oil, divided
1 tbsp. light soy sauce
1 tsp. sesame oil
1 tsp. peeled finely minced fresh ginger
½ tsp. sugar
½ tsp. white sesame seeds
Kosher salt
Ground white pepper

DIRECTIONS:

1. Whisk the eggs with the sesame oil and a pinch each of salt and white pepper in a large bowl, until just combined. Stir the light soy and sugar together to dissolve the sugar entirely in a small bowl. Set aside.
2. Heat a wok over high heat until a drop of water sizzles and evaporates on contact. Add 1 tbsp. of ghee and swirl to coat the base of the wok well. Pour in the egg mixture and swirl and shake the eggs with a heatproof spatula to cook. Take the eggs to a plate when just cooked but not dry.
3. Pour in the remaining 2 tbsps. of ghee to the wok, along with the ginger and garlic. Stir-fry immediately until the garlic and ginger just are fragrant, but take care not to let them burn. Place the rice and soy mixture and stir to combine well. Continue stir-frying, for about 3 minutes. Put the trout and cooked egg and stir-fry to break them up, for about 20 seconds. Then arrange the lettuce and scallions and stir-fry until they are both bright green.
4. Remove from the heat and sprinkle with the sesame seeds. Serve warm.

Vegetable Egg Fried Rice

Prep Time: 10 minutes, Cook Time: 5 minutes, Serves: 4

INGREDIENTS:

4 large eggs, beaten
2 cups cold, cooked rice
1 cup frozen peas, thawed
1 medium carrot, julienned
1 medium onion, diced
1 red bell pepper, diced
4 scallions, cut into ½-inch pieces
2 garlic cloves, crushed and chopped
2 tbsps. cooking oil
1 tbsp. soy sauce
1 tbsp. ginger, crushed and chopped
1 tsp. sesame oil
½ tsp. kosher salt

DIRECTIONS:

1. In a wok, heat the cooking oil over high heat until it shimmers.
2. Add the garlic, ginger, salt and eggs and stir-fry for about 1 minute, or until the eggs are firm.
3. Place the onion, carrot and bell pepper and stir-fry for 1 minute.
4. Toss in the peas, rice, sesame oil, and soy sauce and stir-fry for 1 minute.
5. Top with the scallions and serve hot.

Basic Steamed White Rice

Prep Time: 5 minutes, Cook Time: 25 minutes, Serves: 4 to 6

INGREDIENTS:

3 cups water, plus water for rinsing the rice
2 cups jasmine rice

DIRECTIONS:

1. Add the rice into a wok. Rinse the rice by covering the wok halfway with cold tap water, loosening the starch by running your fingers through the rice, then pouring out the murky water. Repeat this process three or four times, draining as much water as possible. Or you can put the rice in a mesh strainer and rinse it under running tap water.
2. Add 3 cups of water over the rice in the wok.
3. Bring to a boil over high heat, uncovered.
4. While most of the water has been absorbed and you can see the surface of the rice, lower the heat and cover the wok with a lid.
5. Simmer the rice for another 12 minutes. No peeking!
6. Turn off the heat. Let the rice sit, covered, for about 5 minutes.
7. Open the lid. Just before serving, fluff the rice with a spatula or chopsticks.

Japanese Fried Rice with Bacon

Prep Time: 12 minutes, Cook Time: 6 minutes, Serves: 4

INGREDIENTS:

2 cups cold, cooked rice
½ pound (227 g) thick-sliced bacon, cut into 1-inch pieces
3 eggs, beaten
4 scallions, cut into ½-inch pieces
2 garlic cloves, crushed and chopped
2 tbsps. sesame seeds
1 tbsp. ginger, crushed and chopped
1 tsp. sesame oil
Kosher salt
Ground black pepper

DIRECTIONS:

1. In a wok over high heat, stir-fry the bacon, garlic and ginger for about 2 minutes, or till the bacon is lightly browned.
2. Transfer the bacon to a bowl and set aside.
3. Add the eggs and stir-fry until they are firm and dry.
4. Toss in the cooked bacon, rice and sesame oil and stir-fry for about 1 minute.
5. Put the sesame seeds and scallions and toss for 30 seconds.
6. Season with salt and pepper to taste. Serve warm.

Chinese Sausage Fried Rice with Peas

Prep Time: 8 minutes, Cook Time: 5 minutes, Serves: 4

INGREDIENTS:

2 links cured Chinese sausage, sliced into ½-inch pieces
2 large eggs, beaten
2 cups cold, cooked rice
1 cup frozen peas, thawed
4 scallions, cut into ½-inch pieces
2 garlic cloves, crushed and chopped
2 tbsps. soy sauce
1 tbsp. cooking oil
1 tbsp. ginger, crushed and chopped
1 tbsp. sesame oil

DIRECTIONS:

1. In a wok, heat the cooking oil over high heat until it shimmers.
2. Add the garlic, ginger and sausage and stir-fry for about 1 minute.
3. Push the sausage to the sides of the wok, then add the eggs and stir-fry for about 1 minute.
4. Put the peas, rice, soy sauce and sesame oil and stir-fry for 1 minute.
5. Garnish with the scallions and serve warm.

Ginger Congee

Prep Time: 5 minutes, Cook Time: 1 hour, Serves: 4 to 6

INGREDIENTS:

1 cup short-grain rice, rinsed

6 cups water

2-inch piece ginger, peeled

DIRECTIONS:

1. Place the rinsed rice, ginger and 6 cups water in the wok.
2. Bring to a boil over high heat, then reduce the heat to low and simmer, partially uncovered, for about 1 hour, stirring frequently.
3. Serve warm.

Easy Steamed Quinoa

Prep Time: 5 minutes, Cook Time: 20 minutes, Serves: 4 to 6

INGREDIENTS:

2½ cups water

2 cups quinoa, rinsed

DIRECTIONS:

1. Add the rinsed quinoa into a wok, and pour in the water.
2. In the wok over medium-high heat, bring the water to a boil, uncovered.
3. Once the water starts to boil, reduce the heat to low, cover the wok with a lid and cook for about 15 minutes.
4. Turn off the heat and open the wok. Fluff the quinoa using a fork then allow it to sit for 5 minutes before serving.

Indian Fried Rice with Onion

Prep Time: 10 minutes, Cook Time: 4 minutes, Serves: 4

INGREDIENTS:

2 cups cold, cooked basmati rice

¼ cup coarsely chopped mint leaves

1 medium onion, diced

2 garlic cloves, crushed and chopped

2 bird's eye chiles, sliced into ¼-inch circles

2 tbsps. cooking oil

1 tbsp. ginger, crushed and chopped

1 tsp. mustard seeds

1 tsp. hot sesame oil

½ tsp. turmeric

½ tsp. ground coriander

¼ tsp. kosher salt

DIRECTIONS:

1. In a wok, heat the cooking oil over high heat until it

shimmers.

2. Add the onion, ginger, mustard seeds and garlic to the wok and stir-fry for about 1 minute.
3. Place the bird's eye chiles, sesame oil, coriander, turmeric, salt and rice and stir-fry for 1 minute.
4. Sprinkle with the mint and serve hot.

Classic Cambodian House Fried Rice

Prep Time: 10 minutes, Cook Time: 12 minutes, Serves: 4

INGREDIENTS:

4 cups jasmine rice

1 cup frozen sweet peas

1 cup carrot, chopped

¼ head cabbage, chopped

1 onion, chopped

2 garlic cloves, minced

3 tbsps. vegetable oil

1 tbsp. soy sauce

1 tsp. Sriracha sauce

½ tsp. sugar

1 tsp. salt

¼ tsp. ground black pepper

DIRECTIONS:

1. In a wok over high heat, heat the oil.
2. Place the remaining ingredients except the rice and stir to mix well.
3. Add the rice and stir until heated entirely.
4. Enjoy warm.

Simple Sinangag

Prep Time: 10 minutes, Cook Time: 5 minutes, Serves: 4

INGREDIENTS:

2 cups cold, cooked rice

8 cloves garlic, crushed and chopped

4 scallions, cut into

¼-inch pieces

2 tbsps. cooking oil

¼ tsp. kosher salt

DIRECTIONS:

1. In a wok, heat the cooking oil and garlic over medium-high heat. Stir-fry for about 2 minutes until the garlic becomes golden brown but does not burn.
2. Take half the garlic and reserve it for garnishing.
3. Slowly sprinkle the rice and salt into the wok and stir-fry for about 1 minute.
4. Garnish with the chopped scallions and caramelized garlic. Serve warm.

Chicken Chow Mein with Bok Choy, page 30

Beef Lo Mein with Bean Sprouts, page 29

Sesame Noodles with Peanut Butter, page 32

Egg Noodles with Scallions, page 32

Chapter 6: Pasta

Honey Chow Mein with Vegetable

Prep Time: 12 minutes, Cook Time: 6 minutes, Serves: 6

INGREDIENTS:

1 pound (454 g) cooked noodles
2 cups sugar snap or snow pea pods
1 medium onion, cut into 1-inch pieces
1 red bell pepper, cut into 1-inch pieces
4 scallions, cut into 1-inch pieces
2 garlic cloves, crushed and chopped
¼ cup cooking oil
¼ cup hoisin sauce
2 tbsps. honey
2 tbsps. soy sauce
2 tbsps. Shaoxing rice wine
1 tbsp. ginger, crushed and chopped

DIRECTIONS:

1. In a wok, heat the cooking oil over high heat until it shimmers.
2. Add the noodles and stir-fry for about 2 minutes until lightly browned.
3. Take the noodles and drain off all but 2 tbsps. of oil.
4. Place the garlic, ginger and onion to the wok and stir-fry for 1 minute.
5. Put the bell pepper and pea pods and stir-fry for 1 minute.
6. Toss the noodles, honey, hoisin sauce, soy sauce and rice wine and stir-fry for 1 minute.
7. Sprinkle with the scallions and serve warm.

Seafood Lo Mein with Pork

Prep Time: 15 minutes, Cook Time: 6 minutes, Serves: 6

INGREDIENTS:

1 pound (454 g) cooked noodles
¼ pound (113 g) medium shrimp, peeled, deveined, and cut in half lengthwise
¼ pound (113 g) sea scallops, cut in half widthwise
¼ pound (113 g) ground pork
1 medium onion, cut into
1-inch pieces
1 red bell pepper, cut into 1-inch pieces
¼ cup oyster sauce
2 garlic cloves, crushed and chopped
2 tbsps. soy sauce
2 tbsps. rice wine
2 tbsps. cooking oil
1 tbsp. ginger, crushed and chopped

DIRECTIONS:

1. In a wok, heat the cooking oil over high heat until it shimmers.
2. Add the garlic, ginger, pork, and onion and stir-fry for about 1 minute.
3. Place the bell pepper and shrimp and stir-fry for about 1 minute.
4. Put the scallops and stir-fry for about 30 seconds.
5. Whisk together the soy sauce, rice wine and oyster sauce in a small bowl, then pour the mixture to the wok.
6. Toss in the noodles and stir-fry for 30 seconds.
7. Serve hot.

Healthy Vegetable Lo Mein

Prep Time: 6 minutes, Cook Time: 5 minutes, Serves: 2

INGREDIENTS:

8 ounces (227 g) lo mein or egg noodles
water for boiling noodles
SAUCE:
1 tsp. sesame oil
2 tbsps. soy sauce
1 tbsp. dark soy sauce
2 tsps. oyster sauce
1 tsp. brown sugar
STIR-FRY:
6 large whole dried shiitake mushrooms,
soaked and cut into thin strips
4 ounces (113 g) fresh snow peas
1 small carrot, julienned
2 stalks baby bok choy, cut into ½-inch strips
2 tbsps. peanut oil
2-inch piece ginger, peeled and julienned
2 garlic cloves, minced

DIRECTIONS:

1. If using fresh noodles, boil them in a wok over high heat for 30 seconds and drain. If using dried noodles, boil them in a wok over high heat until al dente and drain.
2. Prepare the sauce by combining the soy sauce, dark soy sauce, oyster sauce, brown sugar and sesame oil in a small bowl. Set it aside.
3. In a wok, heat the peanut oil over medium-high heat.
4. Place the ginger and garlic and stir-fry until fragrant, or for about 20 seconds.
5. Put the mushrooms and snow peas. Once the snow peas turn bright green, stir in the carrot and bok choy. Stir-fry until the bok choy leaves are wilted.
6. Remove from the heat and pour in the noodles and sauce. Stir just to combine.
7. Transfer the noodles to a serving dish and serve hot.

Beef Lo Mein with Bean Sprouts

Prep Time: 15 minutes, Cook Time: 20 minutes, Serves: 6

INGREDIENTS:

½ pound (227 g) fresh lo mein egg noodles
½ pound (227 g) beef sirloin tips, sliced across the grain into thin strips
2 cups mung bean sprouts
1 cup snow peas, strings removed
½ red bell pepper, sliced into thin strips
2 garlic cloves, finely minced
2 peeled fresh ginger
slices, each about the size of a quarter
3 tbsps. vegetable oil, divided
2 tbsps. sesame oil, divided
2 tbsps. Shaoxing rice wine
2 tbsps. cornstarch, divided
2 tbsps. dark soy sauce
Kosher salt
Ground white pepper

DIRECTIONS:

1. Bring a pot of water to a boil over high heat and cook the noodles according to package instructions. Reserve ¼ cup of the cooking water and drain the noodles through a colander. Rinse the noodles with cold water and drain excess water again. Drizzle 1 tbsp. of sesame oil over noodles and toss to coat well. Set aside.

2. Stir together the rice wine, 2 tsps. of cornstarch, dark soy, and a generous pinch of white pepper in a mixing bowl. Place the beef and toss to coat. Set aside for about 10 minutes to marinate.

3. Heat a wok over high heat until a drop of water sizzles and evaporates on contact. Add the vegetable oil and swirl to coat the base of the wok well. Season the oil with the ginger and a small pinch of salt. Let the ginger sizzle in the oil for 30 seconds, swirling slowly. Place the beef, reserving the marinade, and sear against the wok for about 2 to 3 minutes. Toss and flip the beef constantly, stir-frying for 1 more minute, or until no longer pink. Take to a bowl and set aside.

4. Pour in the remaining 1 tbsp. of vegetable oil and stir-fry the bell pepper, tossing and flipping for about 2 to 3 minutes, until soft. Put the snow peas and garlic, stir-frying for another minute, or until the garlic is aromatic.

5. Push all the ingredients to the sides of the wok and add the remaining 1 tbsp. of sesame oil, remaining 4 tsps. of cornstarch, reserved marinade, and ¼ cup of the reserved cooking water. Toss together and bring to a boil. Take the beef back to the wok and toss to combine with the vegetables for about 1 to 2 minutes, until the sauce turns thick and glossy.

6. Stir in the lo mein noodles with the beef and vegetables until the noodles are evenly coated with the sauce. Add the bean sprouts and toss to combine well. Scoop out and discard the ginger. Take the noodles to a platter and serve hot.

Shrimp Hor Fun with Gravy

Prep Time: 10 minutes, Cook Time: 8 minutes, Serves: 4 to 6

INGREDIENTS:

GRAVY:
½ cup water
2 cups chicken stock
2 tbsps. soy sauce
3 tbsps. cornstarch
2 tsps. oyster sauce
2 pinches ground white pepper
1 tsp. Shaoxing wine
½ tsp. sugar
STIR-FRY:
1 pound (454 g) fresh flat rice noodles
½ pound (227 g) rice vermicelli noodles,
soaked in warm water for 30 minutes
10 to 12 large shrimp, peeled and deveined
1 stalk choy sum or 2 baby bok choy, cut into 1-inch pieces
1 small carrot, sliced
2 garlic cloves, minced
2 tbsps. peanut oil, plus 2 tsps.
1½ tbsps. soy sauce, divided
¾ tsp. dark soy sauce, divided

DIRECTIONS:

1. Prepare the gravy by mixing the chicken stock, water, cornstarch, soy sauce, oyster sauce, Shaoxing wine, sugar and pepper in a large bowl. Set it aside.

2. In a wok, heat 2 tbsps. of peanut oil over high heat.

3. Place the flat rice noodles and toss in 1 tbsp. of soy sauce and ½ tsp. of dark soy sauce. Stir-fry gently for about 1 minute, being careful not to over-stir so as to allow some parts of the noodles to turn slightly charred. Take the flat noodles from the wok and set them aside.

4. Put the vermicelli noodles, remaining ½ tbsp. of soy sauce and remaining ¼ tsp. of dark soy sauce. Stir-fry for 1 minute.

5. Take the flat rice noodles back to the wok, stirring just to combine with the vermicelli noodles. Remove from the wok and set aside.

6. Reduce the heat to medium-high and drizzle in the remaining 2 tsps. of oil to the wok.

7. Place the garlic and stir-fry for 20 seconds, until fragrant.

8. Add the gravy in the wok. Arrange the shrimp, choy sum, and carrot. Slowly stir and allow the gravy to boil for 1 minute. Remove to a large bowl.

9. When ready to serve, pour the gravy mixture over the fried noodles.

Chicken Chow Mein with Bok Choy

Prep Time: 15 minutes, Cook Time: 15 minutes, Serves: 4

INGREDIENTS:

½ pound (227 g) fresh thin Hong Kong–style egg noodles
½ pound (227 g) chicken thighs, sliced into thin strips
3 heads baby bok choy, cut into bite-sized pieces
1 large handful (2 to 3 ounces / 57 to 85 g) mung bean sprouts
2 garlic cloves, finely minced
¼ cup low-sodium chicken broth
4 tbsps. vegetable oil, divided
1½ tbsps. sesame oil, divided
2 tsps. cornstarch
2 tsps. dark soy sauce
2 tsps. oyster sauce
2 tsps. Shaoxing rice wine
2 tsps. light soy sauce
Ground white pepper

DIRECTIONS:

1. Bring a pot of water to a boil over high heat and cook the noodles according to package instructions. Reserve 1 cup of the cooking water and drain the noodles through a colander. Rinse the noodles under cold water and pour in 1 tbsp. of sesame oil. Toss to coat well and set aside.
2. Combine the rice wine, light soy and a pinch of white pepper in a mixing bowl. Toss the chicken pieces to coat and marinate for about 10 minutes. Stir together the chicken broth, dark soy, remaining ½ tbsp. of sesame oil, oyster sauce, and cornstarch in a small bowl. Set aside.
3. Heat a wok over high heat until a drop of water sizzles and evaporates on contact. Add 3 tbsps. of vegetable oil and swirl to coat the base of the wok well. Arrange the noodles in one layer and fry for about 2 to 3 minutes, or until they are golden brown. Flip the noodles over gently and fry on the other side for another 2 minutes, or until the noodles are crispy and brown, and have formed into a loose cake. Take the noodles to a paper towel–lined plate and set aside.
4. Pour in the remaining 1 tbsp. of vegetable oil and stir-fry the chicken and marinade for about 2 to 3 minutes, until the chicken is no longer pink and the marinade has evaporated. Place the bok choy and garlic, stir-frying until the bok choy stems are soft, about 1 minute.
5. Add the sauce and stir to combine with the chicken and bok choy.
6. Return the noodles and toss the noodles with the chicken and vegetables for about 2 minutes, until coated evenly with the sauce. If the noodles are a bit dry, pour in a tbsp. or so of the reserved cooking water as you toss. Place the bean sprouts and stir-fry, lifting and scooping for 1 more minute.
7. Remove from the heat and serve hot.

Singapore Noodles with Shrimp

Prep Time: 10 minutes, Cook Time: 20 minutes, Serves: 4

INGREDIENTS:

½ pound (227 g) dried rice vermicelli noodles
½ pound (227 g) medium shrimp, peeled and deveined
½ pound (227 g) char shiu (Chinese roast pork), sliced into thin strips
1 cup frozen peas, thawed
1 small white onion, thinly sliced into strips
½ green bell pepper, cut into thin strips
½ red bell pepper, cut into thin strips
8 to 10 fresh cilantro sprigs
2 garlic cloves, finely minced
Juice of 1 lime
3 tbsps. coconut oil, divided
2 tsps. curry powder
1 tsp. fish sauce (optional)
Kosher salt
Freshly ground black pepper

DIRECTIONS:

1. Bring a large pot of water to boil over medium-high heat. Turn off the heat and place the noodles. Soak for about 4 to 5 minutes, until the noodles become opaque. Gently drain the noodles in a colander. Rinse the noodles under cold water and set aside.
2. Season the shrimp with the fish sauce (if using) in a small bowl, and set aside for 5 minutes. If you don't want to use fish sauce, use a pinch of salt to season the shrimp instead.
3. Heat a wok over high heat until a drop of water sizzles and evaporates on contact. Add 2 tbsps. of coconut oil and swirl to coat the base of the wok well. Season the oil with a small pinch of salt. Put the shrimp and stir-fry for about 3 to 4 minutes, or until the shrimp is pink. Remove to a clean bowl and set aside.
4. Pour in the remaining 1 tbsp. of coconut oil and swirl to coat the wok evenly. Stir-fry the bell peppers, onion, and garlic for 3 to 4 minutes, until the onions and peppers are tender. Add the peas and stir-fry until just heated through, about another 1 minute.
5. Arrange the pork and return the shrimp to the wok. Stir together with the curry powder, salt and pepper. Place the noodles and toss to combine well. As you continue to gently toss them with the other ingredients, the noodles will turn a brilliant golden yellow color. Continue stir-frying and tossing for 2 minutes, until the noodles are heated through.
6. Take the noodles to a platter, drizzle with the lime juice, and sprinkle with the cilantro. Serve hot.

Hakka Noodles with Pork and Cabbage

Prep Time: 15 minutes, Cook Time: 6 minutes, Serves: 8

INGREDIENTS:

1 pound (454 g) cooked noodles
1 pound (454 g) ground pork
1 medium carrot, julienned
1 medium onion, diced
1 cup shredded cabbage
2 garlic cloves, crushed and chopped
1 scallion, cut into ½-inch pieces
2 tbsps. cooking oil
1 tbsp. ginger, crushed and chopped
1 tbsp. fish sauce
1 tbsp. soy sauce
1 tbsp. hoisin sauce
1 tsp. hot sesame oil
1 tsp. ground coriander

DIRECTIONS:

1. In a wok, heat the oil over high heat until it shimmers.
2. Add the garlic, ginger and pork and stir-fry for 1 minute.
3. Place the onion, carrot and cabbage and stir-fry for 1 minute.
4. Put the noodles and stir-fry for 1 minute.
5. Toss the soy sauce, fish sauce, hoisin, coriander and sesame oil and stir-fry for 1 minute.
6. Garnish with the scallion and serve warm.

Canton Pancit

Prep Time: 10 minutes, Cook Time: 6 minutes, Serves: 8

INGREDIENTS:

1 pound (454 g) cooked Hong Kong–style noodles
¼ pound (113 g) boneless chicken thighs, cut into 1-inch pieces
¼ pound (113 g) thinly sliced sirloin steak, cut into 1-inch pieces
¼ pound (113 g) medium shrimp, peeled, deveined, and cut in half lengthwise
1 medium onion, cut into 1-inch pieces
1 medium carrot, julienned
4 ounces (113 g) shiitake mushrooms, sliced
¼ cup oyster sauce
¼ cup meat or vegetable broth
4 scallions, cut into 1-inch pieces
Lemon wedges
2 garlic cloves, crushed and chopped
2 tbsps. cooking oil
2 tbsps. soy sauce
1 tbsp. ginger, crushed and chopped
1 tbsp. fish sauce

DIRECTIONS:

1. In a wok, heat the oil over high heat until it shimmers.
2. Add the garlic, ginger, chicken and carrot and stir-fry for 1 minute.
3. Place the steak, mushrooms and onion and stir-fry for 1 minute.
4. Toss the shrimp, soy sauce, fish sauce, oyster sauce, and broth and stir-fry for 1 minute.
5. Add the noodles and stir-fry for 1 minute.
6. Sprinkle with the scallions and serve with the lemon wedges.

Saucy Chicken Chow Mein

Prep Time: 20 minutes, Cook Time: 10 minutes, Serves: 4 to 6

INGREDIENTS:

CHICKEN MARINADE:
1 (5-ounce / 142-g) chicken breast, cut into bite-size pieces
2 tsps. soy sauce
2 tsps. cornstarch
1 tsp. oyster sauce
SAUCE:
1 tbsp. oyster sauce
2 tbsps. soy sauce
2 tsps. Shaoxing wine
1 tsp. sesame oil
1 tsp. brown sugar
½ tsp. salt
2 pinches ground white pepper
STIR-FRY:
2 tbsps. peanut oil, plus more if needed
1 pound (454 g) fresh chow mein noodles or fresh egg noodles, cooked according to package directions
2 cups shredded cabbage
1 small carrot, julienned
2 scallions, cut into 1-inch pieces
2 garlic cloves, minced

DIRECTIONS:

1. In a medium bowl, pour the soy sauce, oyster sauce and cornstarch over the chicken and marinate at room temperature for about 20 minutes.
2. Prepare the sauce by combining the soy sauce, oyster sauce, Shaoxing wine, brown sugar, sesame oil, salt and pepper in a small bowl.
3. In a wok, heat the peanut oil over medium-high heat. Once the wok starts to smoke, place the chicken and stir-fry until entirely cooked. Remove the chicken to a bowl and set it aside.
4. Drizzle in a little more oil to the wok as needed. Put the garlic and stir-fry for about 20 seconds, until fragrant.
5. Arrange the shredded cabbage and carrot, and stir-fry until the cabbage is wilted slightly.
6. Add the noodles with the sauce and take the chicken back to the wok.
7. Stir-fry for 1 minute until combine all the ingredients.
8. Remove from the heat, add the scallions and stir to combine well. Transfer to a serving dish and serve hot.

Sesame Noodles with Peanut Butter

Prep Time: 10 minutes, Cook Time: 4 minutes, Serves: 4

INGREDIENTS:

1 pound (454 g) cooked noodles
4 scallions, cut into ½-inch pieces
2 garlic cloves, crushed and chopped
¼ cup peanut butter
¼ cup peanut oil
2 tbsps. cooking oil
2 tbsps. powdered sugar
2 tbsps. soy sauce
1 tbsp. sesame seeds
1 tbsp. hot sesame oil
1 tbsp. ginger, crushed and chopped

DIRECTIONS:

1. Whisk together the peanut butter, peanut oil, sesame oil, powdered sugar and soy sauce until smooth in a medium bowl. Set aside.
2. In a wok, heat the cooking oil over high heat until it shimmers.
3. Add the garlic, ginger and noodles and stir-fry for about 1 minute.
4. Pour in the peanut butter mixture and toss for about 30 seconds.
5. Sprinkle with the scallions and sesame seeds and serve warm.

Egg Noodles with Scallions

Prep Time: 5 minutes, Cook Time: 15 minutes, Serves: 2

INGREDIENTS:

½ pound (227 g) fresh Chinese egg noodles
8 garlic cloves, finely minced
6 scallions, thinly sliced
6 tbsps. unsalted butter
2 tbsps. sesame oil,
divided
2 tbsps. oyster sauce
2 tbsps. light brown sugar
1 tbsp. light soy sauce
½ tsps. ground white pepper

DIRECTIONS:

1. Bring a pot of water to a boil over high heat and cook the egg noodles according to package directions. Reserve 1 cup of the boiling water, then drain. Drizzle 1 tbsp. of sesame oil over the noodles and toss to coat well. Set aside.
2. Stir together the brown sugar, oyster sauce, light soy and white pepper in a small bowl. Set aside.
3. In a wok over medium-high heat, melt the butter until the foaming stops. Add the minced garlic and half the scallions. Stir-fry for about 30 seconds, or until the garlic is softened.
4. Pour in the sauce and toss to combine with the butter and garlic. Bring the sauce to a simmer and place the noodles. Toss the noodles to coat with

sauce evenly. If the noodles need to loosen up a bit, pour in some of the cooking water, 1 tbsp. at a time. Continue to stir-fry the noodles for about 2 to 3 minutes, until they are heated completely.
5. Remove the noodles to a platter and garnish with the remaining scallions. Serve warm.

Beef Chow Fun with Bean Sprouts

Prep Time: 15 minutes, Cook Time: 5 minutes, Serves: 4 to 6

INGREDIENTS:

BEEF MARINADE:
½ pound (227 g) sirloin steak or tenderloin, cut into thin strips
2 tsps. cornstarch
1 tsp. soy sauce
1 tsp. oyster sauce
Pinch freshly ground black pepper
SAUCE:
2 tbsps. soy sauce
2 tsps. Shaoxing wine
2 tsps. dark soy sauce
½ tsp. brown sugar
Pinch ground white pepper

STIR-FRY:
1 pound (454 g) fresh flat rice noodles (or about 8 ounces / 227 g dried flat noodles, soaked in warm water until al dente)
2 cups fresh bean sprouts, rinsed
½ small onion, cut into thin slices
2 garlic cloves, minced
2 scallions, cut into 1-inch pieces
2 tbsps. peanut oil, divided, plus more if needed

DIRECTIONS:

1. Add the oyster sauce, soy sauce, pepper and cornstarch over the beef, and toss to coat well. Marinate the beef at room temperature for about 15 minutes.
2. Slowly separate the flat rice noodles so they are not clumpy. Pour in some peanut oil over the noodles to loosen them as necessary.
3. Prepare the sauce by mixing together the soy sauce, dark soy sauce, Shaoxing wine, brown sugar, and white pepper in a small bowl. Set it aside.
4. In a wok, heat 1 tbsp. of peanut oil over medium-high heat. Place the beef and stir-fry just until no longer pink. Transfer it to a bowl and set it aside.
5. Pour the remaining 1 tbsp. of oil to the wok, then stir in the garlic and onion. Stir-fry just until the onion turn translucent.
6. Increase the heat to high. Put the flat rice noodles to the wok, separating them, then pour in the sauce. Stir-fry until all the noodles are evenly coated.
7. Take the beef back to the wok. Place the bean sprouts and scallions at the last minute then remove from the heat.
8. Serve hot.

Rice Noodles with Beef and Broccoli

Prep Time: 20 minutes, Cook Time: 10 minutes, Serves: 6

INGREDIENTS:

1½ pounds (680 g) fresh wide rice noodles or dried rice noodles
¾ pound (340 g) flank steak or sirloin tips, sliced across the grain into ⅛-inch-thick slices
1 bunch Chinese broccoli (gai lan), stems sliced diagonally into ½-inch pieces, leaves cut into bite-size pieces
2 large eggs, beaten
4 garlic cloves, thinly sliced
5 tbsps. vegetable oil, divided
2 tbsps. oyster sauce
1 tbsp. light soy sauce
2 tsps. dark soy sauce
2 tsps. cornstarch
2 tsps. fish sauce, divided
½ tsp. sugar
½ tsp. kosher salt
Ground white pepper

DIRECTIONS:

1. Stir together the dark soy, cornstarch, 1 tsp. of fish sauce, salt and a pinch of white pepper in a mixing bowl. Add the beef slices and toss to coat well. Set aside to marinate for about 10 minutes.
2. Stir together the oyster sauce, light soy, remaining 1 tsp. of fish sauce and sugar in another bowl. Set aside.
3. If using fresh rice noodles, rinse them with hot water to keep them separated, and set aside. If using dried rice noodles, cook them according to the package instructions, drain and set aside.
4. Heat a wok over high heat until a drop of water sizzles and evaporates on contact. Add 2 tbsps. of oil and swirl to coat the base of the wok evenly. Transfer the beef to the wok with tongs and reserve the marinade. Sear the beef against the wok for about 2 to 3 minutes, until it's brown and a seared crust develops. Take the beef back to the marinade bowl and stir in the oyster sauce mixture.
5. Pour in 2 more tbsps. of oil and stir-fry the garlic for about 30 seconds. Place the Chinese broccoli stems and stir-fry for about 45 seconds, keeping moving frequently to prevent the garlic from burning.
6. Push the broccoli stems to the sides of the wok, making the bottom of the wok empty. Add the remaining 1 tbsp. of oil and scramble the eggs in the well, then toss them together.
7. Put the noodles, sauce and beef, and toss and flip immediately to combine all of the ingredients, stir-frying for 30 more seconds. Place the broccoli leaves and stir-fry for 30 seconds more, or until the leaves are wilted. Transfer to a platter and serve hot.

Chinese Dan Dan Noodles

Prep Time: 12 minutes, Cook Time: 10 minutes, Serves: 4 to 6

INGREDIENTS:

1 pound (454 g) fresh Chinese egg noodles (or about 8 ounces / 227 g dried noodles), cooked according to package instructions
½ pound (227 g) ground pork
¼ cup unsalted roasted peanuts, chopped
½ cup chicken stock
4 garlic cloves, minced
1 scallion, chopped
½-inch piece ginger, peeled and julienned
1 tbsp. peanut oil, plus 2 tsps.
4 tsps. soy sauce
2 tsps. rice vinegar
1 tsp. ground Sichuan peppercorns
1 tsp. dark soy sauce
½ tsp. brown sugar
Pinch salt
Pinch ground white pepper

DIRECTIONS:

1. Rinse the prepared noodles with cold tap water and drain the noodles through a colander, and distribute them evenly between serving bowls.
2. In a wok, heat 2 tsps. peanut oil over medium heat. Add the ginger and half of the garlic and stir-fry until fragrant, about 20 seconds.
3. Place the ground pork and stir-fry until completely cooked. Add 2 tsps. soy sauce, dark soy sauce, brown sugar, salt, and pepper, mixing to combine well. Distribute the pork mixture evenly among the serving bowls over the noodles.
4. Add the remaining 1 tbsp. peanut oil, Sichuan peppercorns, and the remaining garlic to the wok, and stir-fry for 20 seconds.
5. Pour the chicken stock, rice vinegar, remaining 2 tsps. soy sauce, salt, and pepper nto the wok, then stir to combine well. Remove from the heat and distribute the broth evenly over the pork in each serving bowl.
6. Sprinkle the chopped scallion and peanuts over each bowl. Serve hot.

Stir-Fried Shrimp, page 39

Malaysian Chili Squid and Celery, page 43

Garlic King Crab with Hoisin Sauce, page 41

Shrimp and Pork with Lobster Sauce, page 35

Chapter 7: Fish and Seafood

Shrimp and Pork with Lobster Sauce

Prep Time: 8 minutes, Cook Time: 6 minutes, Serves: 4

INGREDIENTS:

½ pound (227 g) medium shrimp, peeled and deveined
½ pound (227 g) ground pork
2 large eggs, beaten
½ cup thawed frozen peas
4 scallions, cut into ½-inch pieces
3 garlic cloves, crushed and chopped
1 cup chicken stock
2 tbsps. cooking oil
2 tbsps. cornstarch
2 tbsps. soy sauce
1 tbsp. ginger, crushed and chopped
1 tbsp. rice wine
1 tsp. hot sesame oil
1 tsp. sugar

DIRECTIONS:

1. Whisk together the stock, cornstarch, soy sauce, sesame oil, and sugar in a small bowl. Set aside.
2. In a wok, heat the cooking oil over high heat until it shimmers.
3. Add the ginger and garlic and stir-fry for 1 minute.
4. Place the pork, shrimp and rice wine and stir-fry for about 1 minute.
5. Pour the stock mixture to the wok and stir until it thickens and forms a light glaze.
6. Put the peas and the eggs. Let the eggs poach for about 1 minute before stirring gently.
7. Sprinkle with the scallions. Serve warm.

Korean Spicy Stir-Fry Squid

Prep Time: 7 minutes, Cook Time: 5 minutes, Serves: 3

INGREDIENTS:

½ pound (227 g) small to medium squid tentacles and rings, rinsed in cold water
4 ounces (113 g) shiitake mushrooms, cut into slices
2 baby bok choy, leaves separated
1 medium red onion, cut into 1-inch pieces
2 Thai bird's eye chiles, cut into ¼-inch circles
4 scallions, cut into 1-inch pieces
2 garlic cloves, crushed and chopped
2 tbsps. soy sauce
2 tbsps. rice wine
2 tbsps. gochujang
2 tbsps. brown sugar
2 tbsps. cooking oil
1 tbsp. ginger, crushed and chopped
1 tbsp. sesame seeds
1 tsp. hot sesame oil

DIRECTIONS:

1. In a wok, heat the cooking oil over high heat until it shimmers.
2. Add the ginger, garlic and onion and stir-fry for about 1 minute.
3. Place the mushrooms and bok choy and stir-fry for 1 minute.
4. Then put the squid and bird's eye chiles and stir-fry for about 30 seconds.
5. Toss the rice wine, soy sauce, gochujang and brown sugar and stir-fry for about 30 seconds.
6. Pour in the sesame oil, sesame seeds and scallions and stir-fry for about 30 seconds.
7. Serve hot.

Teriyaki Salmon with Sugar Snap

Prep Time: 9 minutes, Cook Time: 6 minutes, Serves: 5

INGREDIENTS:

1 pound (454 g) thick, center-cut salmon fillet, cut into 1-inch pieces
2 cups sugar snap or snow pea pods
4 ounces (113 g) shiitake mushrooms, cut into slices
1 medium onion, diced
2 garlic cloves, crushed and chopped
2 scallions, cut into 1-inch pieces
2 tbsps. cooking oil
2 tbsps. honey
2 tbsps. tamari
2 tbsps. mirin
2 tbsps. rice vinegar
1 tbsp. ginger, crushed and chopped
1 tbsp. sesame seeds
1 tbsp. white miso

DIRECTIONS:

1. Whisk together the tamari, honey, mirin, rice vinegar and miso in a large bowl. Place the salmon, making sure to coat evenly with the marinade, and set aside.
2. In a wok, heat the cooking oil over high heat until it shimmers.
3. Add the ginger, garlic and onion and stir-fry for about 1 minute.
4. Place the mushrooms and pea pods and stir-fry for 1 minute.
5. Then add the marinated salmon, reserving the marinade, and slowly stir-fry for about 1 minute.
6. Toss in the marinade and scallions and slowly stir-fry for 30 seconds.
7. Scatter the sesame seeds on top. Serve hot.

Salmon and Vegetables with Oyster Sauce

Prep Time: 9 minutes, Cook Time: 6 minutes, Serves: 4

INGREDIENTS:

1 pound (454 g) thick, center-cut salmon fillet, cut into 1-inch pieces
2 baby bok choy, leaves separated
1 red onion, cut into 1-inch pieces
1 red bell pepper, cut into 1-inch pieces
½ cup oyster sauce
4 scallions, cut into ½-inch pieces
2 garlic cloves, crushed and chopped
2 tbsps. cooking oil
2 tbsps. rice wine
1 tbsp. crushed and chopped ginger

DIRECTIONS:

1. Whisk together the oyster sauce and rice wine in a large bowl. Add the salmon and allow to marinate while you stir-fry.
2. In a wok, heat the cooking oil over high heat until it shimmers.
3. Add the ginger, garlic and onion and stir-fry for about 1 minute.
4. Place the salmon, reserving the marinade, and slowly stir-fry for about 1 minute.
5. Then put the bell pepper and bok choy and stir-fry for about 1 minute.
6. Pour the reserved marinade and scallions to the wok and slowly stir-fry for about 1 minute. Serve warm.

Seafood and Shredded Root Vegetables

Prep Time: 11 minutes, Cook Time: 5 minutes, Serves: 3

INGREDIENTS:

¼ pound (113 g) medium shrimp, shelled and deveined
¼ pound (113 g) sea scallops, cut in half widthwise
¼ pound (113 g) squid tentacles, rinsed in cold water
2 garlic cloves, crushed and chopped
½ cup julienned carrots
½ cup julienned parsnips
½ cup julienned zucchini
4 scallions, cut into ½-inch pieces
¼ cup hoisin sauce
2 tbsps. cooking oil
1 tbsp. ginger, crushed and chopped

DIRECTIONS:

1. In a wok, heat the cooking oil over high heat until it shimmers.
2. Add the ginger and garlic and stir-fry for about 30 seconds.
3. Place the parsnips, carrots and shrimp and stir-fry for about 1 minute.
4. Put the zucchini and stir-fry for about 30 seconds.
5. Then toss the scallops and stir-fry for 30 seconds, or until the edges are just cracked.
6. Add the squid and stir-fry for about 30 seconds, or until the tentacles are just curled.
7. Toss in the hoisin sauce and stir-fry for 30 seconds.
8. Sprinkle with the scallions and serve warm.

Fried Salt and Pepper Shrimp

Prep Time: 16 minutes, Cook Time: 10 minutes, Serves: 5

INGREDIENTS:

1½ pounds (680 g) large shrimp, peeled and deveined, tails left on
1 cup cornstarch
½ cup vegetable oil
6 garlic cloves, thinly sliced
4 scallions, sliced
diagonally
1 jalapeño pepper, halved and seeded, thinly sliced
1 tbsp. kosher salt
1½ tsps. Sichuan peppercorns

DIRECTIONS:

1. In a small sauté pan or skillet, toast the salt and peppercorns over medium heat until aromatic, shaking and stirring constantly to avoid burning. Remove to a bowl to let cool completely. Use a spice grinder or with a mortar and pestle to grind the salt and peppercorns together. Transfer to a bowl and set aside.
2. Pat the shrimp dry with a paper towel.
3. In a wok over medium-high heat, heat the oil to 375ºF (190ºC), or until it bubbles and sizzles around the end of a wooden spoon.
4. In a large bowl, put the cornstarch. Just before you are ready to fry the shrimp, toss half of the shrimp to coat in the cornstarch and gently shake off any excess cornstarch.
5. Fry the shrimp for about 1 to 2 minutes, until they become pink. Transfer the fried shrimp to a rack set over a baking sheet to drain, by using a wok skimmer. Repeat this process with the remaining shrimp of tossing in cornstarch, frying and transferring to the rack to drain.
6. Once all the shrimp have been cooked, gently remove all but 2 tbsps. of the oil and take the wok back to medium heat. Add the jalapeño, scallions, and garlic and stir-fry until the scallions and jalapeño become bright green and the garlic is **fragrant**. Return the shrimp to the wok, season with the salt and pepper mixture (you may not use it all) and toss to coat well. Take the shrimp to a platter and serve warm.

Whole Steamed Fish with Sizzling Oil

Prep Time: 10 minutes, Cook Time: 22 minutes, Serves: 7

INGREDIENTS:
FISH:
1 whole whitefish, about
2 pounds (907 g), head
on and cleaned
4 peeled fresh ginger
slices, each about the
size of a quarter
½ cup kosher salt, for
cleaning
2 tbsps. Shaoxing rice
wine
3 scallions, sliced into

3-inch pieces
SAUCE:
1 tbsp. sesame oil
2 tbsps. light soy sauce
2 tsps. sugar
SIZZLING GINGER OIL:
2 scallions, thinly sliced
2 tbsps. peeled fresh
ginger finely julienned
into thin strips
3 tbsps. vegetable oil

DIRECTIONS:
MAKE THE FISH:
1. Brush the fish inside and out with the kosher salt.
    Rinse the fish and wipe dry with paper towels.
2. On a plate large enough which can fit into a bamboo
    steamer basket, make a bed with half of each of the
    scallions and ginger. Spread the fish on top and stuff
    the remaining scallions and ginger inside the fish.
    Add the rice wine over the fish.
3. Rinse a bamboo steamer basket and its lid with cold
    water and arrange it in the wok. Add about 2 inches
    of cold water, or until it comes above the bottom rim
    of the steamer by about ¼ to ½ inch, but not so high
    that the water surpasses the bottom of the basket.
    Bring the water to a boil over high heat.
4. Put the plate in the steamer basket and cover. Steam
    the fish over medium heat for about 15 minutes
    (add 2 minutes for every half pound more). Before
    transferring from the wok, poke the fish with a fork
    near the head. If the flesh flakes, it's cooked. If
    the flesh still sticks together, steam for another 2
    minutes.
MAKE THE SAUCE:
5. While the fish is steaming, warm the light soy,
    sesame oil and sugar over low heat in a small pan,
    and set aside.
6. When the fish is cooked, transfer to a clean platter.
    Discard the cooking liquid and aromatics from the
    steaming plate. Add the warm soy sauce mixture
    over the fish. Gently tent with foil to keep it warm
    while you prepare the oil.
MAKE THE SIZZLING GINGER OIL:
7. In a small saucepan over medium heat, heat the
    vegetable oil. Just before it starts to smoke, place half
    of each of the ginger and scallions and fry for about
    10 seconds. Add the hot sizzling oil over the top
    of the fish. Sprinkle with the remaining ginger and
    scallions and serve hot.

Stir-Fried Seafood and Veggies with Rice Noodles

Prep Time: 11 minutes, Cook Time: 15 minutes, Serves: 4

INGREDIENTS:
½ pound (227 g) shrimp
(any size, peeled and
deveined) or fish, cut into
1-inch pieces
½ pound (227 g) dried
vermicelli rice noodles or
bean thread noodles
1 small white onion,
sliced into thin, long
vertical strips
1 large handful snow

peas, strings removed
1 red bell pepper, cut into
1-inch pieces
3 peeled fresh ginger
slices, each about the
size of a quarter
2 large garlic cloves,
finely minced
1 cup vegetable oil,
divided
Kosher salt

DIRECTIONS:
1. Heat a wok over high heat until a drop of water
    sizzles and evaporates on contact. Add 2 tbsps. of oil
    and swirl to coat the base of the wok well. Season
    the oil with the ginger slices and a small pinch of salt.
    Let the ginger sizzle in the oil for 30 seconds, swirling
    slowly.
2. Add the onion and bell pepper and stir-fry
    immediately by tossing and flipping them around in
    the wok with a wok spatula. Season with salt lightly
    and continue to stir-fry for about 4 to 6 minutes, until
    the onion is soft and translucent. Place the snow
    peas and garlic, tossing and flipping until the garlic is
    aromatic, about another minute. Take the vegetables
    to a plate.
3. Heat another 1 tbsp. of oil and put the shrimp or
    fish. Slowly toss and season lightly with a small pinch
    of salt. Stir-fry for about 3 to 4 minutes, or until the
    shrimp becomes pink or the fish begins to flake.
    Return the vegetables and toss everything together
    for another 1 minute. Throw the ginger away and
    transfer the shrimp to a platter. Tent the shrimp with
    foil to keep warm.
4. Wipe out the wok and return to medium-high heat.
    Add the remaining oil (about ¾ cup) and heat to
    375ºF (190ºC), or until it bubbles and sizzles around
    the end of a wooden spoon. Once the oil is at
    temperature, add the dried noodles. They will quickly
    begin to puff and rise from the oil. Flip the cloud of
    noodles over with tongs if you need to fry the top,
    and gently lift from the oil and transfer to a paper
    towel–lined plate to drain and cool.
5. Lightly break the noodles into smaller chunks and
    sprinkle over the stir-fried vegetables and shrimp.
    Serve hot.

Deep-Fried Pepper Squid

Prep Time: 8 minutes, Cook Time: 9 minutes, Serves: 4

INGREDIENTS:

1 pound (454 g) squid tubes and tentacles, cleaned and tubes cut into ⅓-inch rings	kept ice cold
3 cups vegetable oil	2 tbsps. coarsely chopped fresh cilantro
½ cup rice flour	Kosher salt
¾ cup sparkling water,	¼ tsp. freshly ground black pepper

DIRECTIONS:

1. In a wok, pour the oil that should be about 1 to 1½ inches deep. Bring the oil over medium-high heat to 375ºF (190ºC). The oil is at the right temperature while the oil bubbles and sizzles around the end of a wooden spoon when it is dipped in. Pat the squid dry with paper towels.
2. At the same time, stir the rice flour with a pinch of salt and the pepper in a shallow bowl. Whisk in just enough sparkling water to form a thin batter. Gently fold in the squid and, working in batches, use a wok skimmer or slotted spoon to lift up the squid from the batter, shaking off any extra excess. Gently lower into the hot oil.
3. Cook the squid for 3 minutes, until golden brown and crisp. Using a wok skimmer, transfer the calamari to a paper towel–lined plate and season lightly with salt. Repeat this with the remaining squid.
4. Take the squid to a platter and sprinkle with the cilantro. Serve warm.

Coconut Curry Crab with Cilantro

Prep Time: 10 minutes, Cook Time: 13 minutes, Serves: 4

INGREDIENTS:

1 pound (454 g) canned crab meat, drained and picked through to remove shell pieces	a quarter
	2 tbsps. vegetable oil
	1 shallot, thinly sliced
¼ cup chopped fresh cilantro or flat-leaf parsley, for garnish	1 tbsp. curry powder
	1 tbsp. Shaoxing rice wine
1 (13½-ounce / 383-g) can coconut milk	¼ tsp. sugar
	Cooked rice, for serving
2 peeled slices fresh ginger, about the size of	Kosher salt
	Freshly ground black pepper

DIRECTIONS:

1. Heat a wok over high heat until a drop of water sizzles and evaporates on contact. Add the oil and swirl to coat the base of the wok well. Season the oil with the ginger slices and a pinch of salt. Let the ginger sizzle in the oil for about 30 seconds, swirling slowly.
2. Add the shallot and stir-fry for 10 seconds. Place the curry powder and stir until aromatic for another 10 seconds.
3. Toss in the coconut milk, sugar, and rice wine, cover the wok and cook for about 5 minutes.
4. Stir in the crab, cover with the lid and cook until heated through, for about 5 minutes. Open the lid, season to taste with salt and pepper, and discard the ginger. Scoop over the top of a bowl of rice and sprinkle with chopped cilantro.

Thai White Fish and Vegetables

Prep Time: 11 minutes, Cook Time: 7 minutes, Serves: 4

INGREDIENTS:

1 pound (454 g) fresh, firm white fish fillet, cut into 1-inch pieces	4 scallions, cut into 1-inch pieces
3 Thai bird's eye chiles, cut into ¼-inch pieces	2 garlic cloves, crushed and chopped
2 cups chopped bok choy	Juice of 1 lime
1 cup bean sprouts	2 tbsps. cooking oil
1 onion, cut into 1-inch pieces	2 tbsps. rice vinegar
	2 tbsps. brown sugar
1 bruised lower stalk of lemongrass, outer leaves removed and stalk cut into 1-inch pieces	1 tbsp. fish sauce
	1 tbsp. mirin
	1 tbsp. ginger, crushed and chopped
	1 tbsp. cornstarch

DIRECTIONS:

1. Whisk together the fish sauce, mirin, rice vinegar, brown sugar, lime juice, and cornstarch in a large bowl.
2. Add the fish to the bowl and set aside to marinate when preparing the wok.
3. In a wok, heat the cooking oil over high heat until it shimmers.
4. Place the ginger, garlic, lemongrass, and onion and stir-fry for about 1 minute.
5. Remove the lemongrass and discard.
6. Put the bird's eye chiles and stir-fry for about 30 seconds.
7. Take the marinated fish to the wok, reserving the marinade, and slowly stir-fry for about 1 minute.
8. Toss in the bok choy and remaining marinade and slowly stir-fry for about 30 seconds.
9. Squeeze the scallions to bruise them, then scatter over the fish.
10. Garnish with the bean sprouts and serve hot.

Sichuan Mussels and Shrimp

Prep Time: 15 minutes, Cook Time: 6 minutes, Serves: 4

INGREDIENTS:

1 pound (454 g) mussels, cleaned and rinsed
½ pound (227 g) large shrimp, with or without shells
¼ cup oyster sauce
¼ cup rice wine
¼ cup vegetable or meat broth
4 garlic cloves, crushed and chopped
2 tbsps. cooking oil
2 tbsps. Chinese five-spice powder
2 tbsps. ginger, crushed and chopped
1 tbsp. red pepper flakes

DIRECTIONS:

1. In a wok, heat the cooking oil over high heat until it shimmers.
2. Add the ginger and garlic and stir-fry until lightly browned.
3. Place the shrimp and stir-fry for about 1 minute.
4. Pour the rice wine, five-spice powder, red pepper and broth and bring to a boil.
5. Then put the mussels, cover the lid and cook for about 2 minutes, or until the mussels open.
6. Uncover the lid and stir the ingredients for about 1 minute, mixing well.
7. Pour the oyster sauce over the mussels and shrimp. Serve warm.

Stir-Fried Shrimp

Prep Time: 6 minutes, Cook Time: 13 minutes, Serves: 4

INGREDIENTS:

1 pound (454 g) medium-large shrimp, peeled and deveined, tails left on
2 scallions, finely julienned
2 tbsps. vegetable oil
2 tsps. Shaoxing rice wine
Kosher salt

DIRECTIONS:

1. Slice the shrimp in half lengthwise with sharp kitchen scissors or a paring knife, keeping the tail section intact. As the shrimp is stir-fried, slicing it this way will give more surface area and create a unique shape and texture!
2. Pat the shrimp dry with paper towels and keep dry. You can keep the shrimp refrigerated and rolled up in a paper towel, for up to 2 hours before cooking.
3. Heat a wok over high heat until a drop of water sizzles and evaporates on contact. Add the oil and swirl to coat the base of the wok well. Season the oil with a small pinch of salt, and swirl slowly.
4. Place the shrimp all at once to the hot wok. Toss and flip immediately for about 2 to 3 minutes, until the shrimp just becomes pink. Season with another small pinch of salt and pour in the rice wine. Allow the wine to boil off while you continue stir-frying, about another 2 minutes. The shrimp should separate and curl, still attached at the tail.
5. Transfer the shrimp to a serving platter and garnish with the scallions. Serve warm.

Deep-Fried Chili-Garlic Oysters

Prep Time: 15 minutes, Cook Time: 10 minutes, Serves: 5

INGREDIENTS:

1 (16-ounce / 454-g) container small shucked oysters
3 cups vegetable oil
½ cup rice flour
½ cup all-purpose flour, divided
¾ cup sparkling water, chilled
1 small red chili, finely diced
1 small green chili, finely diced
3 large garlic cloves, thinly sliced
1 tsp. sesame oil
1 scallion, thinly sliced
½ tsp. baking powder
¼ tsp. onion powder
Kosher salt
Ground white pepper

DIRECTIONS:

1. Drain the shucked oysters through a colander for about 10 minutes to remove as much extra liquid as possible.
2. Stir together the rice flour, ¼ cup of all-purpose flour, baking powder, a pinch each of salt and white pepper and onion powder in a mixing bowl. Pour in the sparkling water and sesame oil, mix until smooth and set aside.
3. In a wok over medium-high heat, heat the vegetable oil to 375ºF (190ºC), or until it bubbles and sizzles around the end of a wooden spoon.
4. Pat dry the oysters with a paper towel and dredge in the remaining ¼ cup of all-purpose flour. Dip the oysters one at a time in the rice flour batter and gently lower into the hot oil.
5. Fry the oysters for about 3 to 4 minutes, or until golden brown. Take to a wire cooling rack fitted over a baking sheet to drain. Season lightly with salt.
6. Return the oil temperature to 375ºF (190ºC) and fry the chilies and garlic slightly until they are crispy but still brightly colored, about 45 seconds. Lift them out of the oil with a wire skimmer and place on a paper towel–lined plate.
7. Place the oysters on a platter and scatter the garlic and chilies over. Garnish with the sliced scallions and serve hot.

Japanese Miso Cod with Tea Rice

Prep Time: 10 minutes, Cook Time: 20 minutes, Serves: 5

INGREDIENTS:

1 pound (454 g) "captain's cut" (very thick) cod, cut into 4 pieces	pieces, for garnish
	2 tbsps. white miso
2 cups genmaicha green tea	2 tbsps. cooking oil
	2 tbsps. honey
1 cup uncooked rice	2 tbsps. tamari
3 garlic cloves, crushed and chopped	2 tbsps. mirin
	1 tbsp. toasted sesame oil
2 scallions cut into ½-inch	1 tbsp. sesame seeds

DIRECTIONS:

1. Prepare the rice as package directions, using genmaicha green tea instead of water.
2. Whisk together the miso, tamari, mirin, honey and sesame oil in a large bowl. Place the cod and coat evenly with the marinade, then set aside.
3. In a wok, heat the cooking oil over high heat until it shimmers.
4. Add the garlic and stir-fry for about 30 seconds until browned.
5. Place the marinated cod in the wok, reserving the marinade, and fry for about 30 seconds per side, flipping slowly.
6. Toss in the marinade and fry the fish for another 30 seconds on each side.
7. Sprinkle with the sesame seeds and scallions and serve warm.

Sweet Vietnamese Scallops and Cucumbers

Prep Time: 10 minutes, Cook Time: 5 minutes, Serves: 4

INGREDIENTS:

1 pound (454 g) large sea scallops, cut in half widthwise	¼ cup fish sauce
	4 scallions, cut into 1-inch pieces
1 European cucumber, raked and cut into ¼-inch disks	2 garlic cloves, crushed and chopped
	Juice of 1 lime
¼ cup brown sugar	2 tbsps. cooking oil
¼ cup rice wine	1 tsp. hot sesame oil
¼ cup rice vinegar	

DIRECTIONS:

1. Combine the rice wine, fish sauce, brown sugar, and lime juice in a large bowl. Add the scallops to marinate and set aside.
2. In a wok, heat the cooking oil over high heat until it

shimmers.
3. Add the scallions and garlic and stir-fry for about 30 seconds.
4. Place the marinated scallops, reserving the marinade, and stir-fry for about 30 seconds.
5. Then pour the cucumber and marinade to the wok and stir-fry for about 30 seconds.
6. Remove from the heat and toss the cucumbers and scallops with the sesame oil and rice vinegar. Serve warm.

Orange Scallops

Prep Time: 35 minutes, Cook Time: 5 minutes, Serves: 3

INGREDIENTS:

1 pound (454 g) fresh sea scallops, rinsed, muscle removed, and patted dry	Grated zest of 1 orange
	3 tbsps. vegetable oil, divided
¼ cup freshly squeezed orange juice	2 tbsps. cornstarch
	2 tbsps. Shaoxing rice wine, divided
1 large egg white	1 tbsp. light soy sauce
2 scallions, green part only, thinly sliced, for garnish	1 tsp. kosher salt, divided
	Red pepper flakes (optional)

DIRECTIONS:

1. Combine the egg white, cornstarch, 1 tbsp. of rice wine and ½ tsp. of salt in a large bowl, and stir with a small whisk until the cornstarch fully dissolves and is no longer lumpy. Toss in the scallops and refrigerate for about 30 minutes.
2. Remove the scallops from the fridge. Bring a medium pot of water to boil over high heat. Pour in 1 tbsp. of vegetable oil and reduce to a simmer. Add the scallops to the simmering water and cook for about 15 to 20 seconds, stirring constantly until the scallops just become opaque (the scallops will not be completely cooked through). Transfer the scallops to a paper towel–lined baking sheet with a wok skimmer and blot dry with paper towels.
3. Combine the remaining 1 tbsp. of rice wine, light soy, orange juice, orange zest, and a pinch of red pepper flakes (if using) in a glass measuring cup, and set aside.
4. Heat a wok over high heat until a drop of water sizzles and evaporates on contact. Add the remaining 2 tbsps. of oil and swirl to coat the base of the wok well. Season the oil with the remaining ½ tsp. salt.
5. Add the scallops to the wok and swirl in the sauce. Stir-fry the scallops until just cooked through, about 1 minute. Transfer the scallops to a serving dish and garnish with the scallions. Serve warm.

Garlic King Crab with Hoisin Sauce

Prep Time: 12 minutes, Cook Time: 6 minutes, Serves: 6

INGREDIENTS:

2 pounds (907 g) king crab legs, cut into 2-inch sections and left in the shell
1 cup fish or lobster broth
¼ cup hoisin sauce
3 garlic cloves, crushed and chopped
4 scallions, cut into ½-inch pieces
3 tbsps. cooking oil
2 tbsps. rice wine
2 tbsps. cornstarch
2 tbsps. ginger, crushed and chopped

DIRECTIONS:

1. Whisk together the broth, rice wine and cornstarch in a small bowl. Set aside.
2. In a wok, heat the cooking oil over high heat until it shimmers.
3. Add the garlic and ginger and stir-fry for about 1 minute.
4. Place the crab legs and stir-fry for about 1 minute.
5. Pour in the broth mixture and stir-fry for about 1 minute.
6. Toss the hoisin sauce and stir-fry until a glaze forms.
7. Squeeze the scallions to bruise them, then scatter them into the wok to garnish the crab.
8. Serve hot.

Seafood and Vegetables with Oyster Sauce

Prep Time: 13 minutes, Cook Time: 7 minutes, Serves: 5

INGREDIENTS:

¼ pound (113 g) medium shrimp, shelled and deveined
¼ pound (113 g) squid tentacles, rinsed in cold water
¼ pound (113 g) scallops, cut in half widthwise
2 cups sugar snap or snow pea pods
1 cup broccoli florets
4 ounces (113 g) shiitake mushrooms, sliced
1 red bell pepper, cut into 1-inch pieces
1 medium onion, cut into 1-inch pieces
4 garlic cloves, crushed and chopped
¼ cup oyster sauce
¼ cup vegetable or meat broth
2 tbsps. cooking oil
1 tbsp. brown sugar
1 tbsp. cornstarch
1 tsp. hot sesame oil

DIRECTIONS:

1. Whisk together the sesame oil, brown sugar, oyster sauce, broth and cornstarch in a small bowl. Set aside.
2. In a wok, heat the cooking oil over high heat until it shimmers.
3. Add the onion and garlic and stir-fry for about 1 minute.
4. Place the mushrooms, shrimp and broccoli and stir-fry for about 1 minute.
5. Then put the scallops and stir-fry for about 30 seconds.
6. Add the pea pods and bell pepper and stir-fry for about 1 minute.
7. Toss in the squid and stir-fry for about 30 seconds.
8. Drizzle in the sesame oil mixture to the wok and stir-fry until a glaze forms. Serve hot.

Fragrant Mussels in Black Bean Sauce

Prep Time: 10 minutes, Cook Time: 14 minutes, Serves: 6

INGREDIENTS:

2 pounds (907 g) live PEI mussels, scrubbed and debearded
½ bunch fresh cilantro, coarsely chopped
4 large garlic cloves, thinly sliced
2 peeled fresh ginger slices, each about the size of a quarter
2 scallions, cut into 2-inch-long pieces
3 tbsps. vegetable oil
2 tbsps. store-bought black bean sauce
2 tbsps. Shaoxing rice wine
2 tsps. sesame oil
Kosher salt

DIRECTIONS:

1. Heat a wok over high heat until a drop of water sizzles and evaporates on contact. Add the vegetable oil and swirl to coat the base of the wok well. Season the oil with the ginger slices and a small pinch of salt. Let the ginger sizzle in the oil for 30 seconds, swirling slowly.
2. Toss the scallions and garlic and stir-fry for about 10 seconds, or until the scallions are wilted.
3. Place the mussels and toss to evenly coat with the oil. Pour the rice wine down the sides of the wok and toss slightly. Cover the lid and steam for about 6 to 8 minutes, until the mussels are opened.
4. Uncover and pour in the black bean sauce, tossing to coat the mussels. Cover and allow to steam for another 2 minutes. Uncover and pick through, carefully removing any mussels that have not opened.
5. Drizzle in the sesame oil over the mussels. Toss slightly until the sesame oil is fragrant. Discard the ginger, take the mussels to a platter and garnish with the cilantro. Serve warm.

Shrimp with Walnut

Prep Time: 8 minutes, Cook Time: 25 minutes, Serves: 4

INGREDIENTS:

1 pound (454 g) jumbo shrimp, peeled
25 to 30 walnut halves
Nonstick vegetable oil spray
3 cups vegetable oil, for frying
⅓ cup cornstarch
¼ cup mayonnaise
3 tbsps. sweetened condensed milk
2 tbsps. sugar
2 tbsps. water
¼ tsp. rice vinegar
Kosher salt

DIRECTIONS:

1. Line a baking sheet with parchment paper. Lightly spray with cooking spray and set aside.
2. Hold the shrimp on a cutting board curved-side down to butterfly it. Starting from the head area, carefully insert the tip of a paring knife three-quarters of the way into the shrimp. Slice down from the center of the shrimp's back to the tail. Don't cut all the way through the shrimp, and do not cut into the tail area. Open the shrimp like a book and spread it flat slowly. Wipe away the vein (the shrimp's digestive tract) if you see it and rinse the shrimp with cold water, then pat dry with a paper towel. Set aside.
3. In a wok over medium-high heat, heat the oil to 375ºF (190ºC), or until it bubbles and sizzles around the end of a wooden spoon. Fry the walnuts until golden brown, for about 3 to 4 minutes, and transfer the walnuts to a paper towel–lined plate with a wok skimmer. Set aside and turn off the heat.
4. Stir together the sugar and water in a small saucepan and bring to a boil over medium-high heat, stirring occasionally, until the sugar dissolves entirely. Lower the heat to medium and simmer to reduce the syrup for about 5 minutes, or until the syrup turns thick and glossy. Place the walnuts and toss to fully coat them with the syrup. Take the nuts to the prepared baking sheet and set aside to cool. The sugar should harden around the nuts and form a candied shell.
5. Stir together the mayonnaise, condensed milk, rice vinegar and a pinch of salt in a small bowl. Set aside.
6. Bring the wok oil back to 375ºF (190ºC) over medium-high heat. As the oil is heating, lightly season the shrimp with a pinch of salt. In a mixing bowl, toss the shrimp with the cornstarch until coated well. Working in small batches, shake any excess cornstarch off the shrimp and fry in the oil, shifting them quickly in the oil so they don't stick together. Fry the shrimp for about 2 to 3 minutes until golden brown.
7. Remove to a clean mixing bowl and pour the sauce over. Slowly fold until the shrimp are coated evenly.

Place the shrimp on a platter and serve with the candied walnuts.

Garlic Shrimp and Scrambled Eggs

Prep Time: 15 minutes, Cook Time: 10 minutes, Serves: 2

INGREDIENTS:

6 ounces (170 g) medium shrimp, peeled and deveined
4 large eggs, at room temperature
2 cups cold water
2 tbsps. vegetable oil, divided
2 garlic cloves, thinly sliced
2 peeled fresh ginger
slices, each about the size of a quarter
1 bunch chives, cut into ½-inch pieces
2 tbsps. sugar
½ tsp. sesame oil
2 tbsps. kosher salt, plus more for seasoning
Freshly ground black pepper

DIRECTIONS:

1. Whisk the salt and sugar into the water until they dissolve entirely in a large bowl. Place the shrimp to the brine. Cover and refrigerate for about 10 minutes.
2. Drain the shrimp through a colander and rinse. Discard the brine. Arrange the shrimp evenly on a paper towel–lined baking sheet and pat dry.
3. Whisk the eggs with the sesame oil and a pinch each of salt and pepper until combined in another large bowl. Set aside.
4. Heat a wok over high heat until a drop of water sizzles and evaporates on contact. Add 1 tbsp. of vegetable oil and swirl to coat the base of the wok. Season the oil with the ginger and a pinch of salt. Let the ginger sizzle in the oil for about 30 seconds, swirling slowly.
5. Add the garlic and stir-fry slightly to flavor the oil, about 10 seconds. Do not let the garlic brown or burn. Place the shrimp and stir-fry for 2 minutes, until they become pink. Transfer the shrimp to a plate and discard the ginger.
6. Take the wok back to the heat and pour in the remaining 1 tbsp. of vegetable oil. Once the oil is hot, swirl the egg mixture into the wok. Swirl gently and shake the eggs to cook. Put the chives to the pan and continue cooking until eggs are cooked but not dry. Return the shrimp to the pan and toss to combine well. Remove from the heat and serve.

Malaysian Chili Squid and Celery

Prep Time: 6 minutes, Cook Time: 5 minutes, Serves: 2

INGREDIENTS:

½ pound (227 g) small to medium squid tentacles and rings, rinsed in cold water
3 stalks celery, cut diagonally into ¼-inch pieces
2 chiles, cut into ¼-inch pieces
2 garlic cloves, crushed and chopped

½ cup oyster sauce
2 tbsps. cooking oil
2 tbsps. rice wine
1 tsp. hot sesame oil

DIRECTIONS:

1. In a wok, heat the cooking oil over high heat until it shimmers.
2. Add the celery and garlic and stir-fry for about 1 minute.
3. Pour in the squid and rice wine and stir-fry for about 1 minute.
4. Then place the chiles and stir-fry for about 30 seconds.
5. Toss the sesame oil and oyster sauce and stir-fry for about 30 seconds.
6. Serve hot.

Stir-Fried Ginger Fish and Bok Choy

Prep Time: 15 minutes, Cook Time: 11 minutes, Serves: 4

INGREDIENTS:

1 pound (454 g) boneless fish fillets, cut into 2-inch chunks
1 large egg white
3 heads baby bok choy, cut into bite-size pieces
4 peeled fresh ginger slices, about the size of a quarter
1 garlic clove, minced

4 tbsps. vegetable oil, divided
1 tbsp. Shaoxing rice wine
2 tsps. cornstarch
1 tsp. sesame oil
½ tsp. light soy sauce
Kosher salt

DIRECTIONS:

1. Mix together the egg white, rice wine, cornstarch, sesame oil and light soy in a medium bowl. Add the fish to the marinade and stir to coat well. Marinate for about 10 minutes.
2. Heat a wok over high heat until a drop of water sizzles and evaporates on contact. Add 2 tbsps. of vegetable oil and swirl to coat the base of the wok well. Season the oil with a small pinch of salt, and swirl slowly.
3. Gently lift the fish from the marinade with a slotted spoon, and sear in the wok for 2 minutes on each side, until lightly browned on both sides. Take the fish to a plate and set aside.
4. Pour the remaining 2 tbsps. of vegetable oil to the wok. Add a small pinch of salt and the ginger and season the oil, swirling slowly for 30 seconds. Place the bok choy and garlic and stir-fry for about 3 to 4 minutes, tossing frequently, until the bok choy is soft.
5. Take the fish back to the wok and slowly toss together with the bok choy until combined. Season lightly with another pinch of salt. Transfer the fish to a platter, discard the ginger and serve hot.

Seafood Salad, page 45

South American Pasta and Beef Salad, page 47

Steak with Arugula Salad, page 46

Savory Bean and Tomato Salad, page 46

Chapter 8: Salads

Seafood Salad

Prep Time: 12 minutes, Cook Time: 5 minutes, Serves: 3

INGREDIENTS:

1½ cups cooked lobster meat, chopped
2 cups iceberg lettuce, torn
¼ cup feta cheese, crumbled
1 tomato, chopped
½ of avocado, peeled, pitted and chopped
2 tbsps. butter
1 tsp. seafood seasoning

DIRECTIONS:

1. In a wok over medium heat, melt the butter.
2. Place the lobster meat and cook for 2 to 3 minutes or till just heated.
3. Toss in the seafood seasoning and quickly remove from heat.
4. Transfer the lobster meat to a large serving bowl.
5. Put the remaining ingredients except the feta cheese and slowly toss to coat well.
6. Top with the cheese and enjoy!

Tuna and Beans Salad

Prep Time: 10 minutes, Cook Time: 7 minutes, Serves: 8

INGREDIENTS:

¾ pound (340 g) green beans, trimmed and snapped in half
1 (16-ounce / 454-g) can Great Northern beans, drained and rinsed
1 (12-ounce / 340-g) can solid white albacore tuna, drained
1 (2¼-ounce / 64-g) can sliced black olives, drained
¼ medium red onion, thinly sliced
6 tbsps. extra-virgin olive oil
3 tbsps. lemon juice
1 tsp. dried oregano
½ tsp. finely grated lemon zest
Salt, to taste

DIRECTIONS:

1. In a medium wok over high heat, place the green beans, ⅓ cup water and a large pinch of salt and bring to a boil.
2. Cook the beans for 5 minutes.
3. Immediately, take the mixture onto a paper towels lined cookie sheet and set aside to cool.
4. Mix together the Great Northern beans, tuna, olives and onion in a bowl.

5. Add the oil, lemon juice, oregano and lemon zest in another bowl and beat till well combined.
6. Pour dressing over the salad and slowly stir to combine.
7. Serve hot.

Butternut Squash and Bean Salad

Prep Time: 15 minutes, Cook Time: 35 minutes, Serves: 8

INGREDIENTS:

2 (15-ounce / 425-g) cans cannellini beans, drained and rinsed
1 cup peeled, seeded, and diced butternut squash
1 cup chopped baby broccoli
3 slices bacon, cooked and crumbled
1 red onion, chopped
¼ cup chicken stock
3 tbsps. maple syrup, divided
3 tbsps. olive oil, divided
½ tsp. dried thyme leaves

DIRECTIONS:

1. In a wok over low heat, place the cannellini beans and cook till heated through.
2. In a wok over medium heat, heat 1 tbsp. of the olive oil and cook the red onion for 5 minutes.
3. Add 1 tbsp. of the maple syrup and stir to combine well.
4. Reduce the heat to medium-low and simmer for 15 minutes, stirring frequently.
5. Turn off the heat and transfer the onion mixture into beans.
6. In the same wok over medium heat, heat 1 more tbsp. olive oil and cook the butternut squash for 8 minutes. Add 1 tbsp. of the maple syrup and cook for 5 minutes.
7. Remove from the heat and transfer the squash mixture into beans.
8. In the same wok, heat the remaining 1 tbsp. of the olive oil on medium heat and cook the broccoli for 7 minutes.
9. Remove from the heat and transfer the broccoli into beans.
10. Place the chicken stock into the bean mixture and increase the heat to medium-low.
11. Toss in the remaining 1 tbsp. of the maple syrup and thyme and bring to a gentle boil.
12. Simmer till heated completely, stirring slowly. Top with the crumbled bacon.

Simple Myriam's Salad

Prep Time: 5 minutes, Cook Time: 25 minutes, Serves: 2

INGREDIENTS:

2 vine ripened tomatoes   minced
3 large green bell   1 tsp. olive oil
peppers   Salt
1 to 2 garlic cloves,

DIRECTIONS:

1. Arrange the bell peppers on the stove and grill them until they turn black.
2. Take them to a plastic bag and seal it. Allow it to rest for about 5 to 6 minutes.
3. Once the time is up, peel, rinse and chop the peppers.
4. In a wok, heat the oil over medium heat.
5. Toss the tomatoes with peppers and garlic. Cook them for about 3 minutes.
6. Season with a pinch of salt and cook them for about 16 minutes while frequently stirring.
7. Serve your salad warm.

Turkey and Bean Salad

Prep Time: 8 minutes, Cook Time: 15 minutes, Serves: 8

INGREDIENTS:

1 tbsp. vegetable oil   ¼ cup spicy ranch-style
1 pound (454 g) ground   salad dressing
turkey   1 head lettuce, chopped
1 (14-ounce / 397-g) can   1 avocado, peeled,
black beans, drained   pitted, and diced
1 (15-ounce / 425-g) can   1 small white onion,
corn, drained   diced
4 green onions, chopped   1 (1-ounce / 28-g)
(optional)   package taco seasoning
⅓ cup shredded Cheddar   mix
cheese

DIRECTIONS:

1. In a wok over medium heat, heat oil and sauté the white onion for 5 minutes.
2. Break ground turkey into small chunks with your hands.
3. Place the turkey into the wok and cook for 2 to 3 minutes.
4. Add the taco seasoning and cook for 5 to 7 minutes.
5. Turn off the heat and set aside to cool slightly.
6. In a large salad bowl, arrange the lettuce and top with the turkey mixture, followed by the black beans, corn, avocado, green onions, Cheddar cheese and spicy ranch dressing.

Savory Bean and Tomato Salad

Prep Time: 7 minutes, Cook Time: 10 minutes, Serves: 6

INGREDIENTS:

1 (15-ounce / 425-g) can   2 cloves garlic, minced
cannellini beans, drained   3 tbsps. white wine
and rinsed   2 tbsps. olive oil
1 (14½-ounce / 411-g)   2 tbsps. chopped fresh
can diced tomatoes   basil
3 cups arugula   1 tsp. dried sage
¼ cup shaved Parmesan   1 tsp. dried thyme
cheese (optional)   Salt and pepper to taste

DIRECTIONS:

1. In a large wok over medium heat, heat the oil and sauté the garlic for 1 minute.
2. Place the wine, tomatoes, thyme and sage and stir to combine well.
3. Increase the heat to medium-high and cook for about 2 to 3 minutes.
4. Toss the basil, cannellini beans, salt and black pepper and cook for about 3 to 4 minutes.
5. Spread the arugula onto a serving platter and place the beans on top.
6. Garnish with the Parmesan cheese and serve hot.

Steak with Arugula Salad

Prep Time: 7 minutes, Cook Time: 10 minutes, Serves: 4

INGREDIENTS:

4 boneless strip steaks, 1   oil, plus 1 tsp.
to 1¼ inches thick   1 tbsp. fresh-squeezed
8 cups loosely packed   lemon juice
arugula, washed and   1 tbsp. chopped fresh
dried   parsley
3 ounces (85 g)   1 tbsp. chopped fresh
Parmesan cheese, cut   oregano
into thin shavings   Pinch of salt
2 garlic cloves, minced   Fresh coarse ground
5 tbsps. extra virgin olive black pepper

DIRECTIONS:

1. In a small bowl, whisk the 5 tbsps. of olive oil with lemon juice, parsley, garlic, oregano and a pinch each of salt and pepper.
2. In a large wok over medium-high heat, heat 1 tsp. of oil.
3. Sprinkle the steaks strips with some salt and pepper. Cook them for about 7 minutes on each side.
4. Spread the arugula leaves in 4 serving plates then put the steaks strips, lemon dressing and cheese on top. Serve your salads immediately.

Peppery Bean and Spinach Salad

Prep Time: 6 minutes, Cook Time: 25 minutes, Serves: 7

INGREDIENTS:

1 (15-ounce / 425-g) can black beans, drained
1 (10-ounce / 283-g) bag fresh baby spinach
1 (10-ounce / 283-g) can diced tomatoes with green chile
1 onion, thinly sliced
2 cloves garlic, chopped
2 tbsps. extra-virgin olive oil
½ tsp. red pepper flakes
1 tsp. kosher salt
½ tsp. ground black pepper

DIRECTIONS:

1. In a large wok over medium-high heat, heat the oil and cook the onion with salt for 10 to 15 minutes.
2. Toss the red pepper, garlic and black pepper and cook for 1 minute.
3. Stir in the black beans and tomatoes and cook for 5 minutes.
4. Turn off the heat and gently stir in the spinach.
5. Set aside, covered for about 3 minutes.
6. Toss the mixture well and serve quickly.

South American Pasta and Beef Salad

Prep Time: 16 minutes, Cook Time: 14 minutes, Serves: 7

INGREDIENTS:

1 pound (454 g) ground beef
3 cups shredded lettuce
2 cups spiral pasta
2 cups halved cherry tomatoes
1 cup shredded Cheddar cheese
1 (7-ounce / 198-g) bag corn chips
½ cup chopped onion
½ cup French salad dressing
1 (1¼-ounce / 35-g) package taco seasoning
2 tbsps. sour cream

DIRECTIONS:

1. Cook the pasta in salty boiling water for 10 minutes until soft before draining it.
2. In a large wok, cook the ground beef for 10 minutes or until it is no longer pink from the center before stirring in taco seasoning.
3. Coat the mixture of pasta and beef with the lettuce, French dressing, tomatoes, Cheddar cheese, onion and corn chips very thoroughly, then refrigerate for at least 2 hours.
4. Pour some sour cream at the top and serve.

Roasted Red Pepper and Edamame Salad

Prep Time: 10 minutes, Cook Time: 15 minutes, Serves: 12

INGREDIENTS:

1 (16-ounce / 454-g) package frozen shelled edamame (green soybeans)
1 (16-ounce / 454-g) package frozen corn
1 (15-ounce / 425-g) can black beans, rinsed and drained
1 (15-ounce / 425-g) can garbanzo beans, drained
1 (12-ounce / 340-g) jar roasted red peppers, drained and chopped
1 sweet onion, diced
¼ cup chopped fresh cilantro
2 tbsps. freshly squeezed lime juice
1 tsp. ground cumin
1 tsp. smoked sea salt

DIRECTIONS:

1. In a large nonstick wok on medium-high heat, cook the frozen corn for 5 minutes, stirring frequently.
2. Place the onion and cook for 5 minutes.
3. Stir in the garbanzo beans, black beans, edamame, roasted red pepper, cumin and salt and cook for 3 to 5 minutes.
4. Turn off the heat and toss in the cilantro and lime juice.
5. Serve hot.

Chicken and Vegetables Stir-Fry Soup, page 51

Ginger Egg Drop Soup, page 49

Hot and Sour Tofu and Mushroom Soup, page 52

Tomato and Egg Drop Soup, page 53

Chapter 9: Soup and Stew

Stir-Fried Bok Choy, Egg and Tofu Soup

Prep Time: 8 minutes, Cook Time: 6 minutes, Serves: 6

INGREDIENTS:

1 pound (454 g) tofu, well drained, patted dry, and cut into 1-inch pieces
1 cup chopped bok choy
4 eggs, beaten
4 ounces (113 g) mushrooms, cut into slices
1 red bell pepper, cut into ¼-inch pieces
2 quarts vegetable or meat broth
2 garlic cloves, crushed and chopped
2 tbsps. cooking oil
1 tbsp. ginger, crushed and chopped
1 tsp. hot sesame oil

DIRECTIONS:

1. In a wok, heat the cooking oil over high heat until it shimmers.
2. Add the ginger, garlic, and tofu and stir-fry until the tofu begins to brown.
3. Place the bell pepper and stir-fry for about 1 minute.
4. Then put the mushrooms and bok choy and stir-fry for about 30 seconds.
5. Add the sesame oil and broth and bring to a boil.
6. Drizzle the beaten eggs over the broth and allow the eggs to float to the top. Serve hot.

Ginger Egg Drop Soup

Prep Time: 5 minutes, Cook Time: 8 minutes, Serves: 2

INGREDIENTS:

2 large eggs, lightly beaten
4 cups low-sodium chicken broth
2 peeled fresh ginger slices, each about the size of a quarter
2 scallions, thinly sliced, for garnish
2 garlic cloves, peeled
3 tbsps. water
2 tbsps. cornstarch
2 tsps. light soy sauce
1 tsp. sesame oil

DIRECTIONS:

1. In a wok over high heat, combine the broth, garlic, ginger, and light soy and bring to a boil. Reduce to a simmer and cook for about 5 minutes. Remove the ginger and garlic and discard.
2. Mix the cornstarch and water in a small bowl and stir the mixture into the wok. Lower the heat to medium-high and stir for 30 seconds, until the soup thickens.
3. Reduce the heat to a simmer. Dip a fork into the beaten eggs and then drag it through the soup, slowly stirring as you go. Continue to dip the fork into the egg and drag it through the soup to make the egg threads. Once all the egg has been added, simmer the soup undisturbed for a few moments to set the eggs. Drizzle in the sesame oil and scoop the soup into serving bowls. Sprinkle with the scallions and serve.

Hot-Sour Seafood and Vegetables Soup

Prep Time: 15 minutes, Cook Time: 8 minutes, Serves: 4

INGREDIENTS:

¼ pound (113 g) medium shrimp, shelled and deveined
¼ pound (113 g) sea scallops, cut in half widthwise
¼ pound (113 g) white fish (like cod or haddock), cut into 1-inch pieces
¼ pound (113 g) ground pork
1 cup chopped bok choy
4 scallions, cut into ½-inch pieces
½ cup julienned carrots
3 quarts vegetable, fish, or meat broth
¼ cup rice vinegar
2 garlic cloves, crushed and chopped
2 tbsps. cornstarch
1 tbsp. cooking oil
1 tbsp. hot sesame oil
1 tbsp. ginger, crushed and chopped

DIRECTIONS:

1. Whisk together the broth, sesame oil, rice vinegar and cornstarch in a large bowl. Set aside.
2. In a wok, heat the cooking oil over high heat until it shimmers.
3. Add the ginger, garlic and pork and stir-fry for about 1 minute.
4. Place the carrots and stir-fry for about 1 minute.
5. Pour the broth mixture to the wok and stir until the cornstarch dissolves entirely and the broth comes to a boil.
6. Then put the bok choy and allow to cook for about 1 minute.
7. Toss the shrimp, followed by the scallops and fish. Cook for about 2 minutes.
8. Garnish with the scallions and serve warm.

Healthy Pork Congee

Prep Time: 20 minutes, Cook Time: 1½ hours, Serves: 4

INGREDIENTS:

¾ cup jasmine rice, rinsed and drained
6 ounces (170 g) ground pork
2 garlic cloves, minced
10 cups water
2 tbsps. vegetable oil
1 tbsp. light soy sauce,
plus more for serving
2 tsps. peeled minced fresh ginger
2 tsps. Shaoxing rice wine
2 tsps. cornstarch
1 tsp. kosher salt

DIRECTIONS:

1. In a heavy-bottomed pot over high heat, bring the water to a boil. Stir in the salt and rice and reduce the heat to a simmer. Cover and cook, stirring frequently, for about 1½ hours, until the rice has turned to a soft porridge-like consistency.
2. While the congee is cooking, stir together the garlic, ginger, light soy, rice wine, and cornstarch in a medium bowl. Add the pork and let it marinate for about 15 minutes.
3. Heat a wok over high heat until a drop of water sizzles and evaporates on contact. Add the vegetable oil and swirl to coat the base of the wok evenly. Place the pork and stir-fry, tossing and breaking up the meat, for about 2 minutes. To get some caramelization, cook for another 1 to 2 minutes without stirring.
4. Top the congee with the stir-fried pork and serve hot.

Healthy Pork and Egg Drop Soup

Prep Time: 6 minutes, Cook Time: 7 minutes, Serves: 4

INGREDIENTS:

1 pound (454 g) ground pork
4 eggs, beaten
1 cup chopped bok choy
1 ounce (28 g) dried, sliced shiitake or tree ear mushrooms
¼ cup cornstarch
4 scallions, cut into
½-inch pieces
2 garlic cloves, crushed and chopped
3 quarts plus 1¼ cups vegetable or meat broth, divided
1 tbsp. ginger, crushed and chopped

DIRECTIONS:

1. Mix 1 cup of the broth with the cornstarch and stir to form a slurry. Keep aside.
2. In a wok, boil ¼ cup of the broth over high heat.
3. Add the pork, garlic and ginger and cook for about 1 minute.
4. Pour the remaining 3 quarts broth and the

mushrooms to the wok. Bring to a boil.
5. Toss the cornstarch slurry into the boiling broth until the broth thickens.
6. Stir the broth in one direction while drizzling the beaten eggs into the wok.
7. Add the bok choy to the broth and let cook for about 30 seconds.
8. Squeeze the scallions to bruise them, while sprinkling them into the soup.
9. Serve hot.

Sizzling Rice and Shrimp Soup

Prep Time: 20 minutes, Cook Time: 12 minutes, Serves: 4

INGREDIENTS:

10 to 12 medium shrimp, peeled and deveined
1 cup cooked rice
2 baby bok choy heads, chopped into bite-size pieces
4 fresh shiitake mushrooms, stems removed and caps thinly sliced
1 large carrot, peeled and cut into ¼-inch-thick slices
4 cups low-sodium chicken broth
3 cups vegetable oil
2 tsps. sesame oil
2 tsps. light soy sauce
1 tsp. Shaoxing rice wine

DIRECTIONS:

1. Preheat the oven to 300ºF (150ºC). Line a baking sheet with aluminum foil. Spread the rice evenly and bake for about 15 to 20 minutes, until it feels dry. Keep aside to cool.
2. In a soup pot over high heat, bring the chicken broth to a boil. Reduce the heat to medium-high, add the mushrooms and carrot. Pour the light soy, sesame oil and rice wine into the soup and simmer for about 5 minutes.
3. Place the bok choy and bring to a boil over high heat. Turn the heat down to simmer and arrange the shrimp. Stir to distribute the vegetables and shrimp evenly and simmer over low heat while you fry the rice.
4. Add the oil in the wok and the oil should be about 1 to 1½ inches deep. Bring the oil over medium-high heat to 375ºF (190ºC). Dip the end of a wooden spoon into the oil. If the oil bubbles and sizzles around it, the oil is ready.
5. Fry the rice a scoopful at a time, until golden brown and crispy, for about 2 to 3 minutes. Lift the rice in clumps out of the oil and transfer to a paper towel–lined plate with a wire skimmer.
6. When ready to serve, distribute the soup and vegetables among 4 soup bowls. Place the crispy rice on top of each bowl and serve while still sizzling.

Sweet Corn and Chicken Soup

Prep Time: 8 minutes, Cook Time: 12 minutes, Serves: 6 to 8

INGREDIENTS:

2 (14¾-ounce / 418-g) cans cream-style sweet corn
2 cups cooked shredded chicken
2 eggs, lightly beaten
8 cups chicken stock
1 scallion, chopped
3 tsps. cornstarch mixed with 2 tbsps. water (optional)
1 tsp. salt
1 tsp. sesame oil

DIRECTIONS:

1. In a wok, add the corn to the chicken stock and bring to a boil over high heat.
2. Place the shredded chicken, sesame oil and salt. Return to a boil.
3. Stir in the cornstarch mixture (if using) to thicken the soup. Return to a boil.
4. Stir the soup with chopsticks and while stirring, add the beaten eggs into the soup. Swirl faster for a thinner, silky egg consistency; or slower for a thicker, chunky egg consistency.
5. Sprinkle with the chopped scallion and serve warm.

Chicken and Vegetables Stir-Fry Soup

Prep Time: 8 minutes, Cook Time: 5 minutes, Serves: 4

INGREDIENTS:

1 pound (454 g) ground or finely chopped chicken
1 cup chopped bok choy
1 medium onion, diced
1 bell pepper (any color), cut into ½-inch pieces
3 quarts meat or vegetable broth
2 garlic cloves, crushed and chopped
4 scallions, cut into ¼-inch pieces
2 tbsps. cooking oil
1 tbsp. ginger, crushed and chopped
Fresh chopped herbs such as cilantro, mint, parsley, or basil, for garnish

DIRECTIONS:

1. In a wok, heat the cooking oil over high heat until it shimmers.
2. Add the garlic, ginger, chicken, onion, and bell pepper and stir-fry for about 1 minute.
3. Place the bok choy and stir-fry for about 30 seconds.
4. Pour the broth and bring to a gentle boil.
5. Squeeze the scallions to bruise them, while sprinkling them into the soup.
6. Garnish with chopped herbs and serve.

Watercress and Pork Rib Soup

Prep Time: 10 minutes, Cook Time: 4 hours, Serves: 6 to 8

INGREDIENTS:

1 pound (454 g) watercress
½ pound (227 g) pork ribs or pork shoulder, cut into 1-inch pieces
6 to 10 dried red dates
¼ cup dried goji berries
12 cups water, divided
1 tbsp. salt
3 pinches ground white pepper

DIRECTIONS:

1. In a wok over high heat, bring 2 cups of water to a boil. Blanch the pork for 5 minutes. Rinse the pork and the wok, and keep the pork aside.
2. In the wok over high heat, bring the remaining 10 cups of water to a boil.
3. Take the pork back to the wok. Reduce the heat to low and simmer, partially covered, for about 3½ hours.
4. Place the red dates, goji berries, watercress, salt and pepper. Simmer for another 10 minutes, and serve warm.

Hot and Sour Beef and Carrot Soup

Prep Time: 9 minutes, Cook Time: 5 minutes, Serves: 6

INGREDIENTS:

1 pound (454 g) shaved steak
1 medium carrot, julienned
1 medium onion, cut into 1-inch pieces
1 cup chopped bok choy
4 ounces (113 g) mushrooms, sliced
¼ cup rice vinegar
3 quarts vegetable or meat broth
2 garlic cloves, crushed and chopped
2 tbsps. cooking oil
1 tbsp. crushed chopped ginger
1 tsp. hot sesame oil

DIRECTIONS:

1. In a wok, heat the cooking oil over high heat until it shimmers.
2. Add the garlic, ginger and carrot and stir-fry for about 30 seconds.
3. Then place the onion and mushrooms and stir-fry for about 30 seconds.
4. Pour in the broth, sesame oil and rice vinegar and bring to a boil.
5. Put the bok choy and steak and stir for about 30 seconds.
6. Serve hot.

Hot and Sour Noodle with Pork Soup

Prep Time: 7 minutes, Cook Time: 6 minutes, Serves: 4

INGREDIENTS:

8 ounces (227 g) dry vermicelli glass noodles	3 quarts meat or vegetable broth
½ pound (227 g) ground pork	2 garlic cloves, crushed and chopped
4 eggs, cracked into a bowl with yolks unbroken	1 scallion, cut into ½-inch pieces
1 cup chopped bok choy	2 tbsps. cooking oil
1 medium carrot, julienned	1 tbsp. ginger, crushed and chopped
¼ cup rice vinegar	1 tsp. hot sesame oil

DIRECTIONS:

1. In a wok, heat the cooking oil over high heat until it shimmers.
2. Add the garlic, ginger, pork, and carrot and stir-fry for about 1 minute.
3. Pour the broth, noodles, sesame oil and rice vinegar and bring to a boil.
4. Add the eggs into the boiling broth without breaking the yolks and poach for about 1 minute.
5. Scatter the bok choy into the soup and allow it to cook for 1 minute.
6. Sprinkle with the scallion and serve with one egg in each bowl.

Hot and Sour Tofu and Mushroom Soup

Prep Time: 10 minutes, Cook Time: 10 minutes, Serves: 6 to 8

INGREDIENTS:

½ cup diced firm tofu	¼ cup rice vinegar or apple cider vinegar
½ cup dried wood ear mushrooms, soaked and cut into thin strips	4 tbsps. water
	2 tbsps. cornstarch
4 large shiitake mushrooms, soaked then cut into thin strips	2 tbsps. soy sauce
	2 tsps. sesame oil
2 eggs, lightly beaten	2 tsps. brown sugar
¼ cup sliced bamboo shoots	2 tsps. Sichuan chili oil
	1 tsp. dark soy sauce
6 cups chicken stock	2 pinches ground white pepper

DIRECTIONS:

1. In a wok, bring the chicken stock to a boil over medium-high heat.
2. In a small bowl, combine the water and cornstarch and set it aside.

3. Place the soy sauce, dark soy sauce, vinegar, brown sugar, sesame oil, white pepper, and chili oil.
4. Put the tofu, wood ear mushrooms, shiitake mushrooms and bamboo shoots. Bring to a boil.
5. While stirring, slowly pour in the cornstarch mixture. Return to a boil.
6. Stir the soup with chopsticks while slowly pouring the beaten eggs into the soup. The faster you swirl and the faster you pour, the silkier the egg. Swirl and pour slowly for a chunkier egg texture. Serve hot.

Savory Cabbage and Pork Meatball Soup

Prep Time: 15 minutes, Cook Time: 35 minutes, Serves: 8 to 10

INGREDIENTS:

PORK MEATBALLS:	Pinch ground white pepper
½ pound (227 g) ground pork	**SOUP:**
¼ pound (113 g) minced shrimp	½ head napa cabbage, cut into 1-inch pieces
¼ cup finely diced water chestnuts	1 carrot, sliced
	10 cups chicken stock
1½ tbsps. cornstarch	2 tsps. sesame oil
1 tsp. soy sauce	2 tsps. soy sauce
½ tsp. sugar	2 tsps. salt
½ tsp. salt	

DIRECTIONS:

MAKE THE MEATBALLS:

1. Mix the ground pork, shrimp, water chestnuts, soy sauce, sugar, salt, pepper and cornstarch in a bowl. Keep aside to marinate for 15 minutes.

MAKE THE SOUP:

2. In a wok, bring the chicken stock to a boil over high heat.
3. Place the cabbage and carrot and simmer for 30 minutes.
4. Shape about 1 heaping tbsp. of pork mixture into a ball and continue until all the pork mixture is used. Carefully add the meatballs into the boiling soup one at a time. Do not stir. As the meatballs cook, they will rise to the top. They will take 3 minutes to cook through.
5. Add the salt, sesame oil and soy sauce just before removing from the heat.

Tomato and Egg Drop Soup

Prep Time: 10 minutes, Cook Time: 9 minutes, Serves: 6

INGREDIENTS:

2 eggs, lightly beaten
1 medium tomato, diced
4 cups chicken stock
1 scallion, chopped

3 tbsps. water
1½ tbsps. cornstarch
1 tsp. salt
Pinch ground white pepper

DIRECTIONS:

1. Combine the cornstarch and water in a small bowl.
2. In a wok, bring the chicken stock to a boil over medium-high heat. Season with the salt.
3. Stir in the cornstarch-water mixture. Return to a boil.
4. Swirl the soup with a pair of chopsticks, and at the same time slowly pour the beaten eggs into the soup. Swirl faster for a thinner, silky egg consistency; or slower for a thicker, chunky egg consistency.
5. Place the tomato and pepper, stir and simmer for about 1 minute.
6. Sprinkle with the scallion and serve hot.

Lotus Root and Pork Ribs with Goji Soup

Prep Time: 10 minutes, Cook Time: 4 hours, Serves: 6 to 8

INGREDIENTS:

1 pound (454 g) lotus root, peeled and cut into
¼-inch-thick rounds
1 pound (454 g) pork ribs, cut into 1-inch pieces
¼ cup dried goji berries
½ cup dried red dates (optional)

12 cups water
2 tbsps. soy sauce
1 tsp. salt
½ tsp. peppercorns

DIRECTIONS:

1. In a wok, add the pork ribs, lotus root, peppercorns, red dates (if using) and water.
2. Simmer over low heat for at least 4 hours, and up to 6 hours.
3. Remove from the heat and place the soy sauce, salt and goji berries.
4. Let the soup rest for about 15 minutes for the goji berries to reconstitute, then serve warm.

Chicken and Bell Peppers with Black Bean Sauce, page 63

Pepper Fried Chicken, page 63

Kung Pao Chicken with Peanuts, page 56

Broccoli Chicken with Black Bean Sauce, page 55

Chapter 10: Poultry

Garlic Chicken

Prep Time: 9 minutes, Cook Time: 5 minutes, Serves: 4

INGREDIENTS:

1 pound (454 g) boneless chicken thighs, cut into 1-inch pieces
1 medium carrot, roll-cut into ½-inch pieces
1 medium onion, cut into 1-inch pieces
1 red bell pepper, cut into 1-inch pieces
½ cup whole-milk Greek yogurt
2 garlic cloves, crushed and chopped
2 tbsps. ghee
2 tbsps. salted butter
1 tbsp. ginger, crushed and chopped
1 tsp. hot sesame oil
1 tsp. ground cumin
1 tsp. ground coriander
1 tsp. ground paprika
1 tsp. ground cloves

DIRECTIONS:

1. In a wok, heat the ghee over high heat until it shimmers.
2. Add the garlic, ginger, and carrot and stir-fry for 1 minute.
3. Place the chicken, onion, bell pepper, coriander, cumin, paprika and cloves and stir-fry for about 1 minute.
4. Toss the butter and sesame oil and stir-fry for about 1 minute.
5. Remove from the heat and stir in the yogurt.
6. Serve warm.

Coconut Curry Caribbean

Prep Time: 14 minutes, Cook Time: 50 minutes, Serves: 8

INGREDIENTS:

2 pounds (907 g) boneless skinless chicken breasts, cut into ½-inch chunks
1 (14½-ounce / 411-g) can stewed, diced tomatoes
1 (14-ounce / 397-g) can coconut milk
1 (8-ounce / 227-g) can tomato sauce
½ onion, thinly sliced
2 cloves garlic, crushed
3 tbsps. sugar
2 tbsps. curry powder
1½ tbsps. vegetable oil
1 tsp. salt and pepper, or to taste

DIRECTIONS:

1. Evenly season the chicken pieces with the salt and pepper.
2. In a large wok over medium-high heat, heat the oil and curry powder for 2 minutes.
3. Stir in the onions and garlic and cook for 1 minute.
4. Add the chicken and slowly stir to combine well with the curry oil.
5. Turn the heat to medium and cook for 7 to 10 minutes.
6. Stir in the coconut milk, tomato sauce, tomatoes and sugar and simmer, covered for 30 to 40 minutes, stirring from time to time. Serve warm.

Broccoli Chicken with Black Bean Sauce

Prep Time: 15 minutes, Cook Time: 17 minutes, Serves: 7

INGREDIENTS:

1 pound (454 g) broccoli, cut into bite-size florets
¾ pound (340 g) boneless, skinless chicken thighs, cut into 2-inch chunks
4 peeled fresh ginger slices, about the size of a quarter
¼ cup store-bought black bean sauce
2 tbsps. vegetable oil
2 tbsps. water
1 tbsp. Shaoxing rice wine
2 tsps. light soy sauce
1 tsp. minced garlic
1 tsp. cornstarch
¼ tsp. sugar
Kosher salt
Red pepper flakes (optional)

DIRECTIONS:

1. Mix together the rice wine, light soy, garlic, cornstarch and sugar in a small bowl. Add the chicken and marinate for about 10 minutes.
2. Heat a wok over high heat until a drop of water sizzles and evaporates on contact. Add the vegetable oil and swirl to coat the base of the wok well. Add the ginger and a pinch of salt. Let the ginger sizzle for 30 seconds, swirling slowly.
3. Take the chicken to the wok, discarding the marinade. Stir-fry the chicken for about 4 to 5 minutes, until no longer pink. Place the broccoli, water and a pinch of red pepper flakes (if using) and stir-fry for about 1 minute. Cover the wok and steam the broccoli for about 6 to 8 minutes, until it is crisp-tender.
4. Stir in the black bean sauce until coated and heated through, for about 2 minutes, or until the sauce has thickened slightly and become glossy.
5. Scoop out and discard the ginger, then transfer to a platter. Serve hot.

Malaysian Chicken and Bok Choy

Prep Time: 11 minutes, Cook Time: 5 minutes, Serves: 5

INGREDIENTS:

1 pound (454 g) boneless chicken thighs, cut into 1-inch pieces
1 cup chopped bok choy
1 medium red onion, cut into 1-inch pieces
¼ cup sambal oelek
4 scallions, cut into 1-inch pieces
2 garlic cloves, crushed and chopped
2 tbsps. cooking oil
1 tbsp. ginger, crushed and chopped
1 tbsp. fish sauce

DIRECTIONS:

1. In a wok, heat the cooking oil over high heat until it shimmers.
2. Add the garlic, ginger and chicken and stir-fry for about 1 minute.
3. Place the onion and stir-fry for about 1 minute.
4. Then put the sambal oelek and stir-fry for about 30 seconds.
5. Toss the fish sauce and bok choy and stir-fry for about 1 minute.
6. Sprinkle with the scallions and serve warm.

Kung Pao Chicken with Peanuts

Prep Time: 20 minutes, Cook Time: 10 minutes, Serves: 4 to 6

INGREDIENTS:

¾ pound (340 g) boneless, skinless, chicken thighs, cut into 1-inch cubes
6 to 8 whole dried red chilies, or 1 tsp. red pepper flakes
¼ cup unsalted dry roasted peanuts
3 scallions, white and green parts separated, thinly sliced
2 garlic cloves, minced
2 tbsps. vegetable oil
3 tsps. light soy sauce
2½ tsps. cornstarch
2 tsps. Chinese black vinegar
1 tsp. sesame oil
1 tsp. Shaoxing rice wine
1 tsp. peeled minced fresh ginger

DIRECTIONS:

1. Stir together the light soy, cornstarch, black vinegar, rice wine and sesame oil in a medium bowl, until the cornstarch is dissolved. Add the chicken and stir slowly to coat. Marinate for about 10 to 15 minutes, or enough time to prepare the rest of the ingredients.
2. Heat a wok over high heat until a drop of water sizzles and evaporates on contact. Add the vegetable oil and swirl to coat the base of the wok well.
3. Add the chilies and stir-fry for 10 seconds, or until they have just begun to blacken and the oil is slightly aromatic. Place the chicken, reserving the marinade, and stir-fry for about 3 to 4 minutes, until no longer pink.
4. Toss in the garlic, scallion whites, and ginger and stir-fry for 30 seconds. Pour in the marinade and mix to coat the chicken evenly. Toss in the peanuts and cook for extra 2 to 3 minutes, until the sauce turns glossy.
5. Take to a serving plate, sprinkle with the scallion greens and serve warm.

Sweet and Sour Pineapple and Chicken

Prep Time: 13 minutes, Cook Time: 8 minutes, Serves: 6

INGREDIENTS:

1 pound (454 g) boneless chicken thighs, cut into 1-inch pieces
1 (8-ounce / 227-g) can pineapple chunks, drained, juice reserved
2 cups sugar snap or snow pea pods
1 medium red bell pepper, cut into 1-inch pieces
4 scallions, cut into 1-inch pieces
2 garlic cloves, crushed and chopped
¼ cup cooking oil
¼ cup plus 2 tbsps. cornstarch, divided
¼ cup rice vinegar
2 tbsps. ketchup
1 tbsp. ginger, crushed and chopped

DIRECTIONS:

1. Whisk together the rice vinegar, ketchup, pineapple juice, and 2 tbsps. of the cornstarch in a small bowl. Set aside.
2. Toss the remaining ¼ cup of cornstarch in a resealable plastic bag or covered bowl. Coat the chicken with the cornstarch and set aside.
3. In a wok over high heat, heat the cooking oil until it shimmers.
4. Add the garlic and ginger and stir-fry for about 30 seconds to lightly brown.
5. Place the chicken and shallow-fry for about 3 to 4 minutes until lightly browned.
6. Take the chicken from the wok and set aside.
7. Remove and discard all but 2 tbsps. of oil from the wok.
8. Place the pea pods and bell pepper and stir-fry for about 30 seconds.
9. Put the pineapple chunks and stir-fry for about 30 seconds.
10. Pour the rice vinegar mixture and stir until a glaze forms.
11. Take the chicken back to the wok, toss with the other ingredients and garnish with the scallions. Serve hot.

Velvet Chicken and Bamboo Shoots

Prep Time: 15 minutes, Cook Time: 10 minutes, Serves: 6

INGREDIENTS:

¾ pound (340 g) boneless, skinless chicken breasts, cut into bite-size slices
¾ pound (340 g) snow peas or sugar snap peas, strings removed
1 (4-ounce / 113-g) can sliced bamboo shoots, rinsed and drained
2 large egg whites
4 peeled fresh ginger slices, each about the

size of a quarter
3 garlic cloves, minced
⅓ cup low-sodium chicken broth
3½ tbsps. vegetable oil, divided
2 tbsps. cornstarch, plus 1 tsp.
1 tbsp. Shaoxing rice wine
Kosher salt
Ground white pepper

DIRECTIONS:

1. In a mixing bowl, beat the egg whites with a fork or whisk until frothy and the tighter clumps of egg white are foamy. Stir in the 2 tbsps. of cornstarch until blended well and no longer clumpy. Slowly fold in the chicken and 1 tbsp. of vegetable oil and marinate for about 10 minutes or up to 30 minutes.
2. Stir together the chicken broth, rice wine and remaining 1 tsp. of cornstarch in a small bowl, and season with a pinch each of salt and white pepper. Keep aside.
3. Bring a medium saucepan filled with water to a boil over high heat. Pour in ½ tbsp. of oil and reduce the heat to a simmer. Allow the marinade to drain off with a wok skimmer or slotted spoon, transfer the chicken to the boiling water. Give the chicken a quick stir so that the pieces do not clump together. Cook for about 40 to 50 seconds, until the chicken is white on the outside but not cooked through. Drain the chicken through a colander and shake off the excess water. Discard the simmering water.
4. Heat a wok over high heat until a drop of water sizzles and evaporates on contact. Add the remaining 2 tbsps. of oil and swirl to coat the base of the wok well. Season the oil with the ginger slices and salt. Let the ginger sizzle in the oil for 30 seconds, swirling slowly.
5. Place the garlic and bamboo shoots and, using a wok spatula, toss to coat with oil and cook until aromatic, for about 30 seconds. Put the snow peas and stir-fry for 2 minutes until bright green and crisp tender. Arrange the chicken to the wok and swirl in the sauce mixture. Toss to coat well and continue cooking for about 1 to 2 minutes, until the chicken is fully cooked.
6. Take to a platter and discard the ginger. Serve warm.

Sweet-and-Sour Chicken and Water Chestnuts

Prep Time: 10 minutes, Cook Time: 16 minutes, Serves: 5

INGREDIENTS:

¾ pound (340 g) boneless, skinless chicken thighs, cut into bite-size chunks
1 (8-ounce / 227-g) can pineapple chunks, drained, juices reserved
1 (4-ounce / 113-g) can sliced water chestnuts, drained
½ yellow onion, cut into ½-inch pieces
½ red bell pepper, cut into ½-inch pieces
½ green bell pepper, cut into ½-inch pieces
¼ cup low-sodium

chicken broth
4 peeled fresh ginger slices, each about the size of a quarter
3 scallions, thinly sliced, for garnish
3 tbsps. vegetable oil, divided
2 tbsps. light brown sugar
2 tbsps. apple cider vinegar
2 tbsps. ketchup
2 tbsps. water
2 tsps. cornstarch
1 tsp. Worcestershire sauce
Kosher salt

DIRECTIONS:

1. Stir together the cornstarch and water in a small bowl and set aside.
2. Heat a wok over high heat until a drop of water sizzles and evaporates on contact. Add 2 tbsps. of oil and swirl to coat the base of the wok well. Season the oil with the ginger and a pinch of salt. Let the ginger sizzle in the oil for 30 seconds, swirling slowly.
3. Add the chicken and sear against the wok for about 2 to 3 minutes. Flip and toss the chicken, stir-frying for 1 minute more, or until no longer pink. Take to a bowl and keep aside.
4. Add the remaining 1 tbsp. of oil and swirl to coat well. Stir-fry the red and green bell peppers and onion for about 3 to 4 minutes, until tender and translucent. Place the pineapple and water chestnuts and continue to stir-fry for 1 minute. Add the vegetables to the chicken and set aside.
5. Pour the reserved pineapple juice, brown sugar, chicken broth, vinegar, ketchup, and Worcestershire sauce into the wok and bring to a boil over high heat. Keep the heat over medium-high and cook for 4 minutes, until the liquid is reduced by half.
6. Take the chicken and vegetables back to the wok and toss to combine well with the sauce. Give the cornstarch-water mixture a good stir and add to the wok. Toss and flip everything around until the cornstarch begins to thicken the sauce, turning glossy.
7. Scoop out and discard the ginger. Transfer to a platter and sprinkle with the scallions. Serve hot.

Quick Tangerine Zest Chicken

Prep Time: 15 minutes, Cook Time: 18 minutes, Serves: 4

INGREDIENTS:

¾ pound (340 g) boneless, skinless chicken thighs, cut into bite-size pieces
3 large egg whites
3 cups vegetable oil
½ yellow onion, thinly sliced into ¼-inch-wide strips
4 peeled fresh ginger slices, each about the size of a quarter
2 scallions, thinly sliced, for garnish
Peel of 1 tangerine, shredded into ⅛-inch-thick strips

Juice of 2 tangerines (about ½ cup)
2 tbsps. cornstarch
1½ tbsps. light soy sauce, divided
1 tbsp. sesame seeds, for garnish
2 tsps. sesame oil
1 tsp. Sichuan peppercorns, slightly cracked
½ tsp. rice vinegar
¼ tsp. ground white pepper
Light brown sugar
Kosher salt

DIRECTIONS:

1. In a mixing bowl, beat the egg whites with a fork or whisk until frothy and until the tighter clumps are foamy. Stir in the cornstarch, white pepper and 2 tsps. of light soy until well blended. Fold in the chicken and marinate for about 10 minutes.
2. Pour the oil which should be about 1 to 1½ inches deep into the wok. Bring the oil over medium-high heat to 375ºF (190ºC). When you dip the end of a wooden spoon into the oil, the oil is ready if the oil bubbles and sizzles around it.
3. Lift the chicken from the marinade and shake off the excess with a slotted spoon or wok skimmer. Slowly lower into the hot oil. Fry the chicken in batches for about 3 to 4 minutes, or until the chicken is golden brown and crispy on the surface. Transfer to a paper towel–lined plate.
4. Pour out all but 1 tbsp. of oil from the wok and set it over medium-high heat. Swirl the oil to coat the base of the wok evenly. Season the oil with the ginger, peppercorns and a pinch of salt. Let the ginger and peppercorns sizzle in the oil for 30 seconds, swirling slowly.
5. Add the onion and stir-fry, tossing and flipping with a wok spatula for about 2 to 3 minutes, or until the onion is soft and translucent. Place the tangerine peel and stir-fry for 1 minute, or until fragrant.
6. Pour in the tangerine juice, sesame oil, vinegar and a pinch of brown sugar. Bring the sauce to a boil and simmer for 6 minutes, until reduced by half. It should be syrupy and very tangy. Taste and season with salt, if needed.
7. Remove from the heat and add the fried chicken,

tossing to coat with the sauce. Take the chicken to a platter, discard the ginger, and sprinkle with the sliced scallions and sesame seeds. Serve hot.

Ginger Chicken in Sesame Sauce

Prep Time: 15 minutes, Cook Time: 13 minutes, Serves: 4

INGREDIENTS:

1 pound (454 g) boneless, skinless chicken thighs, cut into bite-size pieces
3 large egg whites
3 cups vegetable oil
3 peeled fresh ginger slices, each about the size of a quarter
3 garlic cloves, coarsely chopped
2 scallions, thinly sliced,

for garnish
3 tbsps. cornstarch, divided
¼ cup low-sodium chicken broth
2 tbsps. sesame oil
1½ tbsps. light soy sauce, divided
1 tbsp. sesame seeds, for garnish
Kosher salt
Red pepper flakes

DIRECTIONS:

1. In a mixing bowl, beat the egg whites with a fork or whisk until frothy and the tighter clumps of egg white are foamy. Stir together 2 tbsps. of cornstarch and 2 tsps. of light soy until blended well. Gently fold in the chicken and marinate for about 10 minutes.
2. Add the oil that should be about 1 to 1½ inches deep into the wok. Bring the oil over medium-high heat to 375ºF (190ºC). Dip the end of a wooden spoon into the oil, the oil is ready if the oil bubbles and sizzles around it.
3. Lift the chicken from the marinade with a slotted spoon or wok skimmer and shake off the excess. Slowly lower into the hot oil. Fry the chicken in batches for about 3 to 4 minutes, or until the chicken is golden brown and crispy on the surface. Take to a paper towel–lined plate.
4. Pour out all but 1 tbsp. of oil from the wok and set it over high heat. Swirl the oil to coat the base of the wok well. Season the oil with the ginger and a pinch of salt and red pepper flakes. Let the ginger and pepper flakes sizzle in the oil for 30 seconds, swirling slowly.
5. Place the garlic and stir-fry, tossing and flipping with a wok spatula for about 30 seconds. Stir in the chicken broth, remaining 1 tbsp. of cornstarch and remaining 2½ tsps. of light soy. Simmer for about 4 to 5 minutes, until the sauce thickens and looks glossy. Pour in the sesame oil and stir to combine well.
6. Remove from the heat and add the fried chicken, tossing to coat with the sauce. Scoop out the ginger and discard. Transfer to a platter and sprinkle with the sliced scallions and sesame seeds. Serve warm.

Cashew Chicken with Oyster Sauce

Prep Time: 12 minutes, Cook Time: 7 minutes, Serves: 6

INGREDIENTS:

1 pound (454 g) boneless chicken thighs, cut into 1-inch pieces	1-inch pieces
2 cups sugar snap or snow pea pods	½ cup whole cashews
4 ounces (113 g) sliced mushrooms	¼ cup oyster sauce
1 medium carrot, roll-cut into ½-inch pieces	4 scallions, cut into 1-inch pieces
1 red bell pepper, cut into 1-inch pieces	2 garlic cloves, crushed and chopped
1 medium onion, cut into	2 tbsps. cooking oil
	1 tbsp. ginger, crushed and chopped
	2 tbsps. soy sauce

DIRECTIONS:

1. In a wok, heat the cooking oil over high heat until it shimmers.
2. Add the garlic, ginger and carrot and stir-fry for about 1 minute.
3. Place the chicken and onion and stir-fry for about 1 minute.
4. Put the mushrooms, bell pepper, pea pods and cashews and stir-fry for about 1 minute.
5. Toss the oyster sauce and soy sauce and stir-fry for about 1 minute.
6. Sprinkle with the scallions and serve warm.

Chicken Tikka Masala

Prep Time: 9 minutes, Cook Time: 1 hour, Serves: 6

INGREDIENTS:

4 skinless, boneless chicken breast halves, cut into bite-size pieces	1 tbsp. vegetable oil
1 (14-ounce / 397-g) can tomato sauce	1 tbsp. ground cumin
1 cup heavy whipping cream	1 tbsp. white sugar
1 onion, finely chopped	2 tsps. paprika
4 cloves garlic, minced	1 tsp. ground ginger
2 tbsps. ghee (clarified butter)	½ tsp. curry powder
	½ tsp. ground cinnamon
	¼ tsp. ground turmeric
	1 tsp. salt
	1 tsp. cayenne pepper

DIRECTIONS:

1. In a large wok over medium heat, melt the ghee and cook the onion for 5 minutes.
2. Stir in the garlic and cook for about 1 minute.
3. Toss in the cumin, 1 tsp. of the salt, ginger, cinnamon, cayenne pepper and turmeric and cook for 2 minutes.
4. Pour in the tomato sauce and bring to a boil.
5. Turn the heat to low and simmer for 10 minutes.
6. Stir in the cream, 1 tbsp. of the sugar and paprika and again bring to a simmer.
7. Simmer for 10 to 15 minutes, stirring from time to time.
8. In another wok over medium heat, heat the vegetable oil and sear the chicken pieces and curry powder for 3 minutes.
9. Take the chicken with any pan juices into the sauce and simmer for another 30 minutes. Serve warm.

Quesadillas with Chicken

Prep Time: 6 minutes, Cook Time: 13 minutes, Serves: 4

INGREDIENTS:

4 (12 inch) flour tortillas	thinly sliced
2 skinless, boneless chicken breast halves, cut into strips	2 cloves garlic, minced
2 tomatoes, diced	1 jalapeño pepper, seeded and minced
1 onion, finely chopped	½ onion, thinly sliced
¼ cup sour cream, for topping	2 limes, juiced
1 cup shredded Monterey Jack cheese	2 tbsps. olive oil, divided
1 green bell pepper,	2 tbsps. chopped fresh cilantro
	Salt and pepper to taste

DIRECTIONS:

1. Make the pico de gallo by mixing together the tomatoes, chopped onion, lime juice, cilantro, jalapeño pepper, salt and pepper in a small bowl.
2. In a large wok over high heat, heat 1 tbsp. of the olive oil and sear the chicken until cooked through.
3. Take the chicken into a plate and set aside.
4. In the same wok, heat the remaining 1 tbsp. of the olive oil and cook the sliced onion and green pepper until soft.
5. Toss the minced garlic and cook until aromatic.
6. Stir in half of the pico de gallo and cooked chicken.
7. Set aside, covered to keep the mixture warm.
8. In a heavy wok over medium heat, heat 1 flour tortilla.
9. Arrange ¼ cup of the shredded cheese evenly over the tortilla, followed by ½ of the chicken mixture and ¼ cup of the cheese. Cover with another tortilla.
10. Cook until the bottom of tortillas turns golden brown from both sides.
11. Take the quesadilla from the wok and slice into quarters. Repeat this with the remaining tortillas and filling. Serve with the sour cream and remaining pico de gallo.

Lemongrass Chicken and Bok Choy

Prep Time: 12 minutes, Cook Time: 5 minutes, Serves: 5

INGREDIENTS:

1 pound (454 g) boneless chicken thighs, cut into 1-inch pieces
2 heads baby bok choy, leaves separated
1 medium red onion, cut into 1-inch pieces
4 ounces (113 g) sliced mushrooms
1 medium red bell pepper, cut into 1-inch pieces
2 lemongrass hearts (the bottom 2 inches of the white inner layers), finely minced
2 garlic cloves, crushed and chopped
2 tbsps. cooking oil
1 tbsp. ginger, crushed and chopped
1 tsp. hot sesame oil
1 tsp. fish sauce
Fresh chopped herbs, such as cilantro, mint, or parsley, for garnish

DIRECTIONS:

1. In a wok, heat the cooking oil over high heat until it shimmers.
2. Add the garlic, ginger, lemongrass, and chicken and stir-fry for about 1 minute.
3. Place the onion, mushrooms and bell pepper stir-fry for about 1 minute.
4. Toss the bok choy, sesame oil and fish sauce and stir-fry for about 30 seconds.
5. Sprinkle with chopped herbs of your choice and serve warm.

Coconut Chicken with Green Curry

Prep Time: 11 minutes, Cook Time: 28 minutes, Serves: 4

INGREDIENTS:

1 pound (454 g) skinless, boneless chicken breast halves, cut into 1 inch cubes
2 cups coconut milk
2 green onions with tops, chopped
½ cup cilantro leaves, for garnish
3 cloves garlic, peeled and chopped
2 tbsps. cooking oil
2 tbsps. green curry paste
2 tbsps. dark soy sauce
2 tbsps. white sugar
1 tbsp. fish sauce
1 tbsp. all-purpose flour
1 tsp. fresh ginger, peeled and finely chopped

DIRECTIONS:

1. Evenly Coat the chicken with 1 tbsp. of the dark soy sauce and then with the flour.
2. In a large wok over medium-high heat, heat the oil and sauté the chicken cubes for 5 minutes.
3. Take the chicken into a plate.
4. In the same wok over medium heat, cook the curry paste for 1 minute.
5. Add the green onions, ginger and garlic and cook for 2 minutes.
6. Place the cooked chicken and stir to coat well with the curry mixture.
7. Stir in the coconut milk, 1 tbsp. of the soy sauce, fish sauce and sugar and simmer for 20 minutes.
8. Garnish with the cilantro leaves and serve warm.

Orange Chicken and Sugar Snap

Prep Time: 10 minutes, Cook Time: 9 minutes, Serves: 4

INGREDIENTS:

1 pound (454 g) boneless chicken thighs, cut into 1-inch pieces
2 cups sugar snap or snow pea pods
1 medium red bell pepper, cut into 1-inch pieces
1 medium onion, cut into 1-inch pieces
4 scallions, cut into 1-inch pieces
2 garlic cloves, crushed and chopped
¼ cup plus 2 tbsps. cornstarch, divided
¼ cup orange juice
Zest of 1 orange
¼ cup cooking oil
2 tbsps. rice vinegar
2 tbsps. rice wine
2 tbsps. brown sugar
2 tbsps. soy sauce
1 tbsp. ginger, crushed and chopped
1 tsp. hot sesame oil

DIRECTIONS:

1. Whisk together the orange zest, sesame oil, 2 tbsps. of the cornstarch, the orange juice, rice vinegar, rice wine, brown sugar and soy sauce in a small bowl. Keep aside.
2. Toss the remaining ¼ cup of cornstarch in a resealable plastic bag or covered bowl. Coat the chicken with the cornstarch, ensuring the pieces are evenly coated.
3. In a wok, heat the cooking oil over high heat until it shimmers.
4. Add the garlic and ginger and stir-fry for about 30 seconds.
5. Shallow-fry the chicken for about 3 to 4 minutes until lightly browned.
6. Remove the chicken and keep aside. Remove and discard all but 2 tbsps. of oil from the wok.
7. Add the onion to the wok and stir-fry for about 1 minute.
8. Put the pea pods and bell pepper and stir-fry for about 30 seconds.
9. Pour in the orange juice mixture and stir until a glaze forms.
10. Take the chicken to the wok. Toss and sprinkle with the scallions. Serve warm.

Stir-Fried Chicken and Mushroom

Prep Time: 12 minutes, Cook Time: 5 minutes, Serves: 4

INGREDIENTS:

1 pound (454 g) boneless chicken thighs, cut into 1-inch pieces
2 cups sugar snap or snow pea pods
4 ounces (113 g) sliced mushrooms
1 medium red bell pepper, cut into ½-inch pieces
4 scallions, cut into 1-inch pieces
2 cloves garlic, crushed and chopped
2 tbsps. cooking oil
2 tbsps. sugar
2 tbsps. soy sauce
2 tbsps. rice wine
2 tbsps. rice vinegar
1 tbsp. cornstarch
1 tbsp. ginger, crushed and chopped

DIRECTIONS:

1. Whisk together the soy sauce, rice wine, rice vinegar, sugar and cornstarch in a small bowl. Set aside.
2. In a wok, heat the cooking oil over high heat until it shimmers.
3. Add the garlic, ginger, and chicken and stir-fry for about 1 minute.
4. Add the mushrooms, pea pods and bell pepper and stir-fry for about 1 minute.
5. Stir the soy sauce mixture into the wok and stir until a light glaze forms.
6. Sprinkle with the scallions and serve hot.

Cilantro-Lime Chicken and Pineapple

Prep Time: 13 minutes, Cook Time: 6 minutes, Serves: 6

INGREDIENTS:

1 pound (454 g) boneless chicken thighs, cut into 1-inch pieces
1 (8-ounce / 227-g) can of pineapple chunks, drained, juice reserved
2 cups sugar snap or snow pea pods
1 medium onion, cut into 1-inch pieces
1 medium red bell pepper, cut into 1-inch pieces
1 cup chopped cilantro
2 garlic cloves, crushed and chopped
Zest and juice of 1 lime
2 tbsps. cooking oil
2 tbsps. fish sauce
1 tbsp. cornstarch
1 tbsp. ginger, crushed and chopped

DIRECTIONS:

1. Whisk together the pineapple juice, lime zest and juice, fish sauce and cornstarch in a small bowl. Set aside.
2. In a wok, heat the cooking oil over high heat until it shimmers.
3. Add the garlic, ginger and chicken and stir-fry for about 1 minute.
4. Place the onion and stir-fry for about 1 minute.
5. Then put the pea pods and bell pepper and stir-fry for about 1 minute.
6. Take the pineapple chunks to the wok and stir-fry for about 1 minute.
7. Pour the pineapple and lime juice mixture to the wok and stir until a light glaze forms.
8. Sprinkle with the cilantro and serve warm.

Cashew Chicken and Zucchini

Prep Time: 20 minutes, Cook Time: 12 minutes, Serves: 4 to 6

INGREDIENTS:

¾ pound (340 g) boneless, skinless, chicken thighs, cut into 1-inch cubes
1 small zucchini, cut into ½-inch pieces
½ cup unsalted dry roasted cashews
½ red bell pepper, cut into ½-inch pieces
2 garlic cloves, minced
2 scallions, white and green parts separated, thinly sliced
½-inch piece peeled finely minced fresh ginger
2 tbsps. vegetable oil
1 tbsp. light soy sauce
2 tsps. Shaoxing rice wine
2 tsps. cornstarch
1 tsp. sesame oil
½ tsp. ground Sichuan peppercorns
Kosher salt

DIRECTIONS:

1. Stir together the light soy, rice wine, cornstarch, sesame oil and Sichuan pepper in a medium bowl. Add the chicken and stir slowly to coat. Allow it to marinate for about 15 minutes, or for enough time to prepare the rest of the ingredients.
2. Heat a wok over high heat until a drop of water sizzles and evaporates on contact. Add the vegetable oil and swirl to coat the base of the wok well. Season the oil with the ginger and a pinch of salt. Let the ginger sizzle in the oil for 30 seconds, swirling slowly.
3. Lift the chicken from the marinade with tongs and transfer to the wok, reserving the marinade. Stir-fry the chicken for about 4 to 5 minutes, until no longer pink. Place the zucchini, red bell pepper and garlic and stir-fry for about 2 to 3 minutes, or until the vegetables are soft.
4. Add the marinade and mix to coat the other ingredients evenly. Bring the marinade to a boil and continue to stir-fry for about 1 to 2 minutes, until the sauce becomes thick and glossy. Stir in the cashews and cook for 1 minute.
5. Transfer to a serving plate, sprinkle with the scallions and serve warm.

Cilantro Chicken Cutlets with Salsa

Prep Time: 5 minutes, Cook Time: 10 minutes, Serves: 4

INGREDIENTS:

4 boneless skinless chicken breast halves
½ cup prepared salsa
¼ cup chopped fresh
cilantro
2 tbsps. fresh lime juice
1 tbsp. Dijon mustard
1 tbsp. butter

DIRECTIONS:

1. Place each chicken breast between 2 plastic wrap sheets and pound into ½-inch thickness with a meat mallet.
2. Evenly brush mustard over each breast.
3. In a large wok over medium heat, melt the butter and cook the chicken for 3 to 4
4. minutes per side.
5. Stir in the salsa and lime juice and simmer, uncovered for 6 to 8 minutes.
6. Sprinkle with the cilantro and serve warm.

Ramen and Chicken Stir-Fry

Prep Time: 11 minutes, Cook Time: 18 minutes, Serves: 3

INGREDIENTS:

8 ounces (227 g) skinless, boneless chicken breast, halves, cut into 2-inch strips
1 (3-ounce / 85-g) package Oriental-flavor ramen
1 Roma tomato, cut into wedges
2 cups broccoli florets
1 cup sliced onion wedges
1 cup fresh bean sprouts
½ cup sliced water chestnuts
2 cloves garlic, minced
1½ cups hot water
½ cup water
2 tsps. vegetable oil, divided
1 tsp. soy sauce
1 tsp. oyster sauce
¼ tsp. chili-garlic sauce, or to taste

DIRECTIONS:

1. Cook ramen noodles in boiling water for 2 minutes and drain it in a colander.
2. Then cook chicken in hot oil for 5 minutes and keep it aside in a bowl.
3. In the same wok, add the broccoli, garlic and onion and cook for about 3 minutes. Place the noodles, water, chili garlic sauce, oyster sauce, bean sprouts, water chestnuts, soy sauce and seasoning from the ramen noodle package.
4. Cook for about 5 minutes before putting tomato wedges and cooking it for 3 more minutes. Serve warm.

Curry Chicken and Potato

Prep Time: 20 minutes, Cook Time: 50 minutes, Serves: 8

INGREDIENTS:

1 (3-pound / 1.4-kg) chicken, cut into pieces
5 russet potatoes, peeled and cut into 1-inch pieces
2 onions, chopped
8 cloves garlic, chopped
¼ cup vegetable oil
¼ cup mild curry powder
2 tbsps. hot curry powder
1 tsp. ground black pepper
Salt to taste

DIRECTIONS:

1. In a large pan over high heat, add the chicken and enough water to cover and bring to a boil.
2. Turn the heat to medium and simmer for 20 minutes.
3. At the same time, heat the vegetable oil over medium heat in a large wok and cook the garlic and onion for 5 minutes.
4. Stir in both curry powders, salt and black pepper and cook for 5 minutes.
5. Take the onion mixture into the pan with the chicken.
6. Toss the potatoes and simmer for 20 minutes.

Curry Coconut Chicken

Prep Time: 7 minutes, Cook Time: 30 minutes, Serves: 2

INGREDIENTS:

2 skinless, boneless chicken breast halves, cut into bite-size pieces
1 small onion, chopped
1 cup plain yogurt
¾ cup coconut milk
½ lemon, juiced
2 cloves garlic, minced
3 tbsps. olive oil
3 tbsps. curry powder
1 tbsp. tomato paste
1 bay leaf
1 tsp. ground cinnamon
1 tsp. paprika
½ tsp. grated fresh ginger root
½ tsp. white sugar
½ tsp. cayenne pepper
Salt to taste

DIRECTIONS:

1. In a large wok over medium heat, heat the olive oil and cook the onion until browned.
2. Stir in the garlic, curry powder, paprika, cinnamon, bay leaf, sugar, ginger and salt and cook for 2 minutes.
3. Place the chicken pieces, tomato paste, yogurt and coconut milk and bring to a boil.
4. Lower the heat and simmer for 20 to 25 minutes.
5. Discard the bay leaf and pour in lemon juice and cayenne pepper.
6. Simmer for 5 minutes.
7. Serve warm.

Pepper Fried Chicken

Prep Time: 5 minutes, Cook Time: 12 minutes, Serves: 8

INGREDIENTS:

2½ to 3 pounds (1.1 to 1.4 kg) chicken pieces
¾ cup all-purpose flour
½ cup canola oil
½ tsp. paprika
½ tsp. garlic salt
½ tsp. celery salt
½ tsp. salt
½ tsp. pepper

DIRECTIONS:
1. Mix together all the ingredients except the chicken and the canola oil in a shallow dish.
2. Place the chicken pieces and coat them with the mixture evenly.
3. In a large wok over high heat, heat the oil to 365ºF (185ºC) and fry the chicken pieces until golden brown.
4. Take the chicken pieces onto paper towel lined plates to drain. Serve warm.

Indian Inspired Curry Chicken

Prep Time: 16 minutes, Cook Time: 30 minutes, Serves: 8

INGREDIENTS:

2 pounds (907 g) skinless, boneless chicken breast halves
1 (15-ounce / 425-g) can crushed tomatoes
1½ cups chopped onion
1 cup plain yogurt
½ cup water, plus 1 tbsp. water
½ cup cooking oil
2 tbsps. chopped fresh cilantro, divided
3 tsps. salt, divided
1½ tsps. minced fresh ginger root
1 tbsp. curry powder
1 tbsp. fresh lemon juice
1 tbsp. minced garlic
1 tsp. garam masala
1 tsp. ground cumin
1 tsp. ground turmeric
1 tsp. ground coriander
1 tsp. cayenne pepper

DIRECTIONS:
1. Evenly season the chicken breasts with 2 tsps. of the salt.
2. In a large wok over high heat, heat the oil and cook the chicken breasts in the batches till browned fully.
3. Take the chicken breasts into a plate and set aside.
4. In the same wok over medium-high heat, cook the garlic, onion and ginger for 8 minutes.
5. Stir in the curry powder, turmeric, cumin, coriander, cayenne and 1 tbsp. of the water and cook for 1 minute.
6. Stir in the yogurt, tomatoes and 1 tbsp. of the chopped cilantro and the remaining 1 tsp. of the salt.
7. Place the cooked chicken breasts and the remaining ½ cup of the water and bring to a boil, turning the chicken occasionally to coat with the sauce.
8. Sprinkle 1 tbsp. of the cilantro and garam masala over the chicken and simmer, covered for 20 minutes.
9. Drizzle in the lemon juice and serve warm.

Chicken and Bell Peppers with Black Bean Sauce

Prep Time: 15 minutes, Cook Time: 10 minutes, Serves: 4

INGREDIENTS:

¾ pound (340 g) boneless, skinless chicken thighs, cut into bite-size pieces
1 small yellow onion, cut into bite-size pieces
½ red bell pepper, cut into bite-size pieces
½ yellow or green bell pepper, cut into bite-size pieces
⅓ cup store-bought black bean sauce
3 garlic cloves, chopped
1 peeled fresh ginger slice, about the size of a quarter
3 tbsps. vegetable oil, divided
1 tbsp. light soy sauce
1 tsp. sesame oil
1 tsp. cornstarch
Kosher salt

DIRECTIONS:
1. Stir the light soy, sesame oil, and cornstarch together in a large bowl, until the cornstarch dissolves. Place the chicken and toss to coat in the marinade. Keep the chicken aside to marinate for about 10 minutes.
2. Heat a wok over high heat until a drop of water sizzles and evaporates on contact. Add 2 tbsps. of vegetable oil and swirl to coat the base of the wok well. Season the oil with the ginger and a pinch of salt. Let the ginger sizzle in the oil for 30 seconds, swirling slowly.
3. Transfer the chicken to the wok and discard the marinade. Allow the pieces to sear in the wok for about 2 to 3 minutes. Flip to sear on the other side for another 1 to 2 minutes more. Stir-fry by tossing and flipping around in the wok immediately for extra 1 minute. Transfer to a clean bowl.
4. Pour in the remaining 1 tbsp. of oil and stir in the bell peppers and onion. Quickly stir-fry for about 2 to 3 minutes, tossing and flipping the vegetables with a wok spatula until the onion turns translucent but is still firm in texture. Place the garlic and stir-fry for about 30 seconds.
5. Take the chicken back to the wok and place the black bean sauce. Toss and flip until the chicken and vegetables are coated evenly.
6. Transfer to a platter, discard the ginger and serve warm.

Chicken and Vegetables with Hoisin Sauce

Prep Time: 8 minutes, Cook Time: 5 minutes, Serves: 6

INGREDIENTS:

1 pound (454 g) ground chicken
2 cups sugar snap or snow pea pods
1 medium carrot, roll-cut into ½-inch pieces
1 medium onion, cut into 1-inch pieces

¼ cup hoisin sauce
2 garlic cloves, crushed and chopped
2 tbsps. cooking oil
1 tbsp. ginger, crushed and chopped

DIRECTIONS:

1. In a wok, heat the cooking oil over high heat until it shimmers.
2. Add the garlic, ginger, carrot and chicken and stir-fry for about 1 minute.
3. Place the onion and pea pods and stir-fry for about 1 minute.
4. Toss the hoisin sauce and stir-fry for about 30 seconds.
5. Serve hot.

Kadai Chicken with Yogurt

Prep Time: 10 minutes, Cook Time: 5 minutes, Serves: 4

INGREDIENTS:

1 pound (454 g) boneless chicken thighs, cut into 1-inch pieces
½ cup whole-milk Greek yogurt
1 medium carrot, roll-cut into ½-inch pieces
1 medium onion, cut into 1-inch pieces
2 chiles, sliced into ¼-inch circles (no need to core or seed them)

2 garlic cloves, crushed and chopped
2 tbsps. ghee
1 tbsp. ginger, crushed and chopped
1 tsp. ground coriander
1 tsp. paprika
1 tsp. cumin

DIRECTIONS:

1. In a wok, heat the ghee over high heat until it shimmers.
2. Add the garlic, ginger, carrot and chicken and stir-fry for about 1 minute.
3. Place the onion, cumin, coriander and paprika and stir-fry for about 1 minute.
4. Then put the sliced chiles and stir-fry for about 1 minute.
5. Remove from the heat and stir the yogurt into the wok. Serve hot.

Sweet and Sour Pork and Pineapple, page 66

Korean Garlic Pork with Kimchi, page 72

Pork and Bok Choy with Oyster Sauce, page 74

Pork and Brussels Sprouts with Oyster Sauce, page 75

Chapter 11: Pork, Beef and Lamb

Cumin Lamb with Cilantro

Prep Time: 10 minutes, Cook Time: 5 minutes, Serves: 4

INGREDIENTS:

1 pound (454 g) boneless leg of lamb or shoulder, cut into 1-inch pieces
1 medium onion, diced
1 red bell pepper, cut into ½-inch pieces
½ cup coarsely chopped
2 garlic cloves, crushed and chopped
2 tbsps. cooking oil
2 tbsps. soy sauce
1 tbsp. ground cumin or cumin seeds
1 tbsp. ginger, crushed and chopped
1 tbsp. rice wine
1 tbsp. rice vinegar
1 tbsp. cornstarch
¼ tsp. kosher salt
½ tsp. ground black pepper

DIRECTIONS:

1. In a wok, heat the cooking oil over high heat until it shimmers.
2. Add the garlic, ginger and lamb and stir-fry for about 1 minute.
3. Place the cumin, onion, salt and black pepper and stir-fry for about 1 minute.
4. Put the bell pepper and stir-fry for about 1 minute.
5. Pour the rice vinegar, rice wine, soy sauce and cornstarch and stir until a glaze is formed.
6. Sprinkle with the cilantro and serve warm.

Sichuan Pork and Bell Pepper with Peanuts

Prep Time: 8 minutes, Cook Time: 5 minutes, Serves: 4

INGREDIENTS:

1 pound (454 g) ground pork
1 medium onion, cut into 1-inch pieces
1 medium red bell pepper, cut into 1-inch pieces
½ cup peanuts
2 garlic cloves, crushed and chopped
2 tbsps. cooking oil
2 tbsps. rice wine
2 tbsps. rice vinegar
1 tbsp. ginger, crushed and chopped
1 tbsp. Chinese five-spice powder
1 tbsp. cornstarch
1 tsp. red pepper flakes
1 tsp. hot sesame oil

DIRECTIONS:

1. In a wok, heat the cooking oil over high heat until it shimmers.
2. Put the garlic, ginger, pork and onion and stir-fry for about 2 minutes.
3. Place the red pepper flakes, five-spice powder, sesame oil and bell pepper and stir-fry for about 1 minute.
4. Toss the rice vinegar, rice wine and cornstarch and stir until a glaze is formed.
5. Add the peanuts and give a stir. Serve warm.

Sweet and Sour Pork and Pineapple

Prep Time: 15 minutes, Cook Time: 6 minutes, Serves: 5

INGREDIENTS:

1 pound (454 g) pork tenderloin, cut into 1-inch pieces
1 (8-ounce / 227-g) can pineapple chunks, drained, juice reserved
1 medium red onion, cut into 1-inch pieces
1 red bell pepper, cut into 1-inch pieces
4 scallions, cut into 1-inch pieces
2 garlic cloves, crushed and chopped
¼ cup cooking oil
¼ cup rice vinegar
¼ cup plus 2 tbsps. cornstarch, divided
2 tbsps. brown sugar
1 tbsp. ginger, crushed and chopped

DIRECTIONS:

1. Whisk together the reserved pineapple juice, rice vinegar, 2 tbsps. of the cornstarch, and brown sugar in a small bowl. Set aside.
2. Put the pork to a resealable plastic bag or covered bowl. Toss with the remaining ¼ cup of cornstarch to coat fully.
3. In a wok, heat the cooking oil over high heat until it shimmers.
4. Add the garlic and ginger and stir-fry for about 1 minute.
5. Place the pork and shallow-fry until lightly browned. Remove the pork and keep aside.
6. Remove and discard all but 2 tbsps. of oil from the wok.
7. Arrange the onion to the wok and stir-fry for about 1 minute.
8. Then put the bell pepper and pineapple chunks and stir-fry for about 1 minute.
9. Pour in the pineapple juice mixture and stir until a glaze is formed. Stir in the cooked pork.
10. Sprinkle with the scallions and serve warm.

Pineapple Pork and Chiles

Prep Time: 10 minutes, Cook Time: 6 minutes, Serves: 4

INGREDIENTS:

1 pound (454 g) pork tenderloin, cut into 1-inch pieces

1 (8-ounce / 227-g) can pineapple chunks, drained, juice reserved

1 medium onion, cut into 1-inch pieces

2 chiles, cut into ¼-inch circles (no need to remove seeds or core)

4 scallions, cut into 1-inch pieces

2 garlic cloves, crushed and chopped

¼ cup rice vinegar

2 tbsps. cooking oil

2 tbsps. brown sugar

2 tbsps. cornstarch

1 tbsp. ginger, crushed and chopped

1 tsp. hot sesame oil

DIRECTIONS:

1. Whisk together the pineapple juice, rice vinegar, brown sugar and cornstarch in a small bowl. Set aside.
2. In a wok, heat the cooking oil over high heat until it shimmers.
3. Add the garlic, ginger and pork and stir-fry for about 1 minute.
4. Put the chiles and onion and stir-fry for about 1 minute.
5. Place the pineapple chunks and sesame oil and stir-fry for about 30 seconds.
6. Pour in the pineapple juice mixture and stir until a glaze is formed.
7. Sprinkle with the scallions and serve warm.

Thai Coconut Curry Lamb

Prep Time: 8 minutes, Cook Time: 5 minutes, Serves: 5

INGREDIENTS:

1 pound (454 g) boneless lamb leg or shoulder, cut into 1-inch pieces

2 cups chopped bok choy

4 ounces (113 g) mushrooms, sliced

1 medium onion, cut into 1-inch pieces

¼ cup canned coconut milk

1 bird's eye chile, thinly sliced

2 garlic cloves, crushed and chopped

2 tbsps. coconut oil

1 tbsp. red Thai curry paste

1 tbsp. ginger, crushed and chopped

1 tbsp. fish sauce

1 tbsp. brown sugar

1 tbsp. cornstarch

DIRECTIONS:

1. Whisk together the curry paste, coconut milk, brown sugar, fish sauce and cornstarch in a small bowl. Keep aside.
2. In a wok, heat the coconut oil over high heat until it shimmers.
3. Add the garlic, ginger and lamb and stir-fry for about 1 minute.
4. Place the mushrooms, onion and bird's eye chile and stir-fry for about 1 minute.
5. Put the bok choy and stir-fry for about 30 seconds.
6. Toss the curry paste mixture and stir until a glaze is formed.
7. Serve warm.

Chinese Tomato and Beef Stir-Fry

Prep Time: 15 minutes, Cook Time: 10 minutes, Serves: 4

INGREDIENTS:

¾ pound (340 g) flank or skirt steak, cut against the grain into ¼-inch-thick slices

5 large tomatoes, each cut into 6 wedges

4 peeled fresh ginger slices, each about the size of a quarter

2 garlic cloves, finely minced

2 scallions, white and green parts separated, thinly sliced

1 large shallot, thinly sliced

2 tbsps. vegetable oil

2 tbsps. light soy sauce

2 tbsps. water

1½ tbsps. cornstarch, divided

1 tbsp. Shaoxing rice wine

1 tbsp. tomato paste

1 tsp. sesame oil

1 tsp. sugar

Kosher salt

Ground white pepper

DIRECTIONS:

1. Mix the beef with 1 tbsp. of cornstarch, rice wine, a small pinch each of salt and white pepper in a small bowl. Keep aside for about 10 minutes.
2. Stir together the remaining ½ tbsp. of cornstarch, light soy, tomato paste, sesame oil, sugar and water in another small bowl. Keep aside.
3. Heat a wok over high heat until a drop of water sizzles and evaporates on contact. Add the vegetable oil and swirl to coat the base of the wok well. Season the oil with the ginger and a pinch of salt. Let the ginger sizzle in the oil for 30 seconds, swirling slowly.
4. Take the beef to the wok and stir-fry for about 3 to 4 minutes, until no longer pink. Place the shallot and garlic and stir-fry for about 1 minute. Put the tomatoes and scallion whites and continue to stir-fry for another 2 to 3 minutes, or until the tomatoes begin to break down slightly.
5. Stir in the sauce and continue to stir-fry for about 1 to 2 minutes, or until the beef and tomatoes are coated evenly and the sauce has thickened slightly.
6. Scoop out and discard the ginger, then transfer to a platter. Garnish with the scallion greens. Serve warm.

Lime Lamb and Chiles

Prep Time: 11 minutes, Cook Time: 5 minutes, Serves: 4

INGREDIENTS:

1 pound (454 g) lamb tenderloin, cut into 1-inch pieces, across the grain
2 or 3 Thai bird's eye chiles
1 medium onion, diced
Juice of 1 lime
4 scallions, cut into 1-inch pieces
2 garlic cloves, crushed and chopped
2 tbsps. cooking oil
1 tbsp. hot sesame oil
1 tbsp. brown sugar
1 tbsp. ginger, crushed and chopped
1 tbsp. cornstarch
1 tbsp. fish sauce
1 tbsp. soy sauce

DIRECTIONS:

1. Whisk together the lime juice, brown sugar, sesame oil and cornstarch in a small bowl. Keep aside.
2. Combine the soy sauce and fish sauce in a large bowl. Add the lamb and massage for about 1 minute.
3. In a wok, heat the cooking oil over high heat until it shimmers.
4. Add the garlic, ginger and lamb and stir-fry for about 1 minute.
5. Place the bird's eye chiles and onion and stir-fry for about 1 minute.
6. Pour in the lime juice mixture and stir until a glaze is formed.
7. Sprinkle with the scallions and serve warm.

Five-Spice Pork and Tofu

Prep Time: 11 minutes, Cook Time: 6 minutes, Serves: 5

INGREDIENTS:

½ pound (227 g) ground pork
½ pound (227 g) extra-firm tofu, cut into 1-inch cubes
1 medium carrot, roll-cut into ½-inch pieces
1 medium onion, cut into 1-inch pieces
1 medium red bell pepper, cut into 1-inch pieces
4 garlic cloves, crushed and chopped
4 scallions, cut into 1-inch pieces
2 tbsps. cooking oil
2 tbsps. soy sauce
2 tbsps. rice wine
1 tbsp. cornstarch
1 tbsp. ginger, crushed and chopped
1 tsp. Chinese five-spice powder

DIRECTIONS:

1. Whisk together the soy sauce, rice wine and cornstarch in a small bowl. Keep aside.
2. In a wok, heat the cooking oil over high heat until it shimmers.
3. Add the carrot, tofu, ginger and garlic and stir-fry for about 2 minutes.
4. Place the pork, onion, and five-spice powder and stir-fry for about 1 minute.
5. Then put the bell pepper and stir-fry for about 1 minute.
6. Pour in the soy sauce mixture and stir until a glaze is formed.
7. Sprinkle with the scallions and serve warm.

Mongolian Garlic Beef

Prep Time: 15 minutes, Cook Time: 10 minutes, Serves: 4

INGREDIENTS:

¾ pound (340 g) flank steak, cut against the grain into ¼-inch-thick slices
4 or 5 whole dried red Chinese chilies
½ yellow onion, thinly sliced
4 garlic cloves, coarsely chopped
1 cup vegetable oil
¼ cup low-sodium chicken broth
2 tbsps. Shaoxing rice wine
2 tbsps. coarsely chopped fresh cilantro
1 tbsp. cornstarch, divided
1 tbsp. dark soy sauce
1 tbsp. light brown sugar
1 tsp. peeled finely minced fresh ginger

DIRECTIONS:

1. Stir together the rice wine, dark soy and 1 tbsp. of cornstarch in a mixing bowl. Place the sliced flank steak and toss to coat well. Keep aside and marinate for about 10 minutes.
2. Add the oil into a wok and bring it over medium-high heat to 375ºF (190ºC). Dip the end of a wooden spoon into the oil, the oil is ready if the oil bubbles and sizzles around it.
3. Lift the beef from the marinade, reserving the marinade. Put the beef to the oil and fry for about 2 to 3 minutes, until it develops a golden crust. Transfer the beef to a clean bowl with a wok skimmer and set aside. Pour in the chicken broth and brown sugar to the marinade bowl and stir to combine well.
4. Discard all but 1 tbsp. of oil from the wok and set it over medium-high heat. Place the chili peppers, ginger and garlic. Let the aromatics sizzle in the oil for 10 seconds, swirling slowly.
5. Put the onion and stir-fry for about 1 to 2 minutes, or until the onion is tender and translucent. Pour in the chicken broth mixture and toss to combine well. Simmer for 2 minutes, then add the beef and toss everything together for extra 30 seconds.
6. Take the beef to a platter, garnish with the cilantro, and serve warm.

Beef with Sha Cha

Prep Time: 9 minutes, Cook Time: 5 minutes, Serves: 4

INGREDIENTS:

1 pound (454 g) sirloin steak, sliced into ¼-inch strips
2 cups sugar snap or snow pea pods
1 medium onion, cut into 1-inch pieces
¼ cup sha cha
1 chile, cut into ¼-inch circles
4 scallions, cut into 1-inch pieces
2 cloves garlic, crushed and chopped
2 tbsps. cooking oil
2 tbsps. soy sauce
2 tbsps. Chinese rice wine
1 tbsp. ginger, crushed and chopped

DIRECTIONS:

1. In a wok, heat the cooking oil over high heat until it shimmers.
2. Add the garlic, ginger, steak and onion and stir-fry for about 1 minute.
3. Pour the rice wine, soy sauce, sha cha and chile and stir-fry for about 1 minute.
4. Place the pea pods and scallions and stir-fry for about 1 minute.
5. Serve warm.

Myanmarese Ham Bowl

Prep Time: 5 minutes, Cook Time: 6 minutes, Serves: 2

INGREDIENTS:

½ pound (227 g) Smithfield ham, cut into ½-inch pieces
2 chiles, cut into ¼-inch circles (no need to core or seed)
2 garlic cloves, crushed and chopped
4 scallions, cut into ½-inch pieces
¼ cup rice wine
¼ cup sriracha
2 tbsps. cooking oil
2 tbsps. brown sugar
2 tbsps. soy sauce
1 tbsp. ginger, crushed and chopped
1 tbsp. cornstarch
1 tsp. hot sesame oil
Fresh chopped cilantro, for garnish

DIRECTIONS:

1. Whisk together the rice wine, cornstarch and brown sugar in a small bowl. Set aside.
2. In a wok, heat the cooking oil over high heat until it shimmers.
3. Add the garlic, ginger and ham and stir-fry for about 1 minute.
4. Place the chiles, soy sauce, sesame oil and sriracha and stir-fry for about 1 minute.
5. Pour the rice wine mixture and stir until a glaze is formed.

6. Put the scallions and stir-fry for about 30 seconds.
7. Top with the cilantro and serve warm.

Sichuan Beef with Carrot and Celery

Prep Time: 17 minutes, Cook Time: 10 minutes, Serves: 4

INGREDIENTS:

¾ pound (340 g) flank or skirt steak, cut against the grain into ¼-inch-thick slices
1 large carrot, peeled and julienned to 3-inch strips
2 celery stalks, julienned to 3-inch strips
4 peeled fresh ginger slices, each about the size of a quarter
3 garlic cloves, lightly crushed
2 scallions, thinly sliced
2 tbsps. vegetable oil
2 tbsps. Shaoxing rice wine
2 tbsps. cornstarch, divided
1 tbsp. dark soy sauce
1 tbsp. hoisin sauce
2 tsps. sesame oil
2 tsps. light soy sauce
2 tsps. water
1 tsp. Sichuan peppercorns, crushed
¼ tsp. Chinese five spice powder

DIRECTIONS:

1. Stir together the rice wine, dark soy and sesame oil in a mixing bowl. Place the beef and toss to combine well. Keep aside for about 10 minutes. Combine the hoisin sauce, water, light soy, 1 tbsp. of cornstarch, and five spice powder in a small bowl. Keep aside.
2. Heat a wok over high heat until a drop of water sizzles and evaporates on contact. Add the vegetable oil and swirl to coat the base of the wok well. Season the oil with the peppercorns, ginger, and garlic. Let the aromatics sizzle in the oil for 10 seconds, swirling slowly.
3. Toss the beef in the remaining 1 tbsp. of cornstarch to coat, and put it to the wok. Sear the beef against the side of the wok for about 1 to 2 minutes, or until a golden-brown seared crust develops. Gently flip and sear on the other side for another minute. Toss and flip for 2 minutes more, until the beef is no longer pink.
4. Move the beef to the sides of the wok and place the celery and carrot to the center. Stir-fry, tossing and flipping until the vegetables are soft, for extra 2 to 3 minutes. Toss in the hoisin sauce mixture and pour into the wok. Continue to stir-fry, coating the beef and vegetables evenly with the sauce for about 1 to 2 minutes, until the sauce begins to thicken and turns glossy. Scoop out the ginger and garlic and discard.
5. Take the beef to a platter and sprinkle with the scallions. Serve warm.

Sesame Pork and Carrot

Prep Time: 8 minutes, Cook Time: 5 minutes, Serves: 4

INGREDIENTS:

1 pound (454 g) pork tenderloin, cut into 1-inch pieces	pieces
	2 garlic cloves, crushed and chopped
1 medium carrot, roll-cut into ½-inch pieces	2 tbsps. cooking oil
	2 tbsps. sesame seeds
1 medium onion, cut into 1-inch pieces	2 tbsps. soy sauce
	2 tbsps. honey
1 medium red bell pepper, cut into 1-inch pieces	1 tbsp. cornstarch
	1 tbsp. ginger, crushed and chopped
4 scallions, cut into 1-inch	1 tsp. hot sesame oil

DIRECTIONS:

1. In a wok, heat the cooking oil over high heat until it shimmers.
2. Add the garlic, ginger and carrot and stir-fry for about 1 minute.
3. Place the pork and stir-fry for about 1 minute.
4. Then put the onion and bell pepper and stir-fry for about 1 minute.
5. Pour the sesame oil, honey, soy sauce and cornstarch and stir until a light glaze is formed.
6. Sprinkle with the sesame seeds and scallions. Serve warm.

Sichuan Beef and Sugar Snap

Prep Time: 12 minutes, Cook Time: 6 minutes, Serves: 5

INGREDIENTS:

1 pound (454 g) sirloin steak, cut into ¼-inch strips	2 tbsps. rice wine
	2 tbsps. rice vinegar
2 cups sugar snap or snow pea pods	2 tbsps. soy sauce
	1 tbsp. ginger, crushed and chopped
1 medium onion, diced	1 tbsp. Chinese five-spice powder
4 scallions, cut into 1-inch pieces	1 tbsp. cornstarch
2 garlic cloves, crushed and chopped	1 tsp. red pepper flakes
	1 tsp. hot sesame oil
2 tbsps. cooking oil	

DIRECTIONS:

1. Whisk together the rice wine, rice vinegar, soy sauce and cornstarch in a small bowl. Keep aside.
2. In a wok, heat the cooking oil over high heat until it shimmers.
3. Add the garlic, ginger and steak and stir-fry for about 1 minute.
4. Place the onion, five-spice powder and red pepper flakes and stir-fry for about 1 minute.
5. Add the pea pods and sesame oil and stir-fry for about 1 minute.
6. Pour in the rice wine mixture and stir-fry until a glaze is formed.
7. Top with the scallions and serve warm.

Fried Pork Loin Chops with Onion

Prep Time: 18 minutes, Cook Time: 14 minutes, Serves: 4

INGREDIENTS:

4 boneless pork loin chops	2 tbsps. cornstarch
	2 tbsps. light soy sauce
1 medium yellow onion, thinly sliced	1 tbsp. Shaoxing wine
	1 tsp. dark soy sauce
3 cups vegetable oil	½ tsp. red wine vinegar
3 peeled fresh ginger slices, each about the size of a quarter	½ tsp. freshly ground black pepper
	Kosher salt
2 garlic cloves, finely minced	Sugar

DIRECTIONS:

1. Use a meat mallet to pound the pork chops until they are ½ inch thick. Place in a bowl and season with the rice wine, a small pinch of salt and pepper. Marinate for about 10 minutes.
2. Add the oil that should be about 1 to 1½ inches deep into the wok. Bring the oil over medium-high heat to 375ºF (190ºC). Dip the end of a wooden spoon into the oil, the oil is ready if the oil bubbles and sizzles around it.
3. Coat the chops with the cornstarch, working in 2 batches. Slowly lower them one at a time into the oil and fry for about 5 to 6 minutes, until golden. Take to a paper towel–lined plate.
4. Discard all but 1 tbsp. of oil from the wok and set it overhigh heat. Season the oil with the ginger and a pinch of salt. Let the ginger sizzle in the oil for 30 seconds, swirling slowly.
5. Stir-fry the onion for 4 minutes, until translucent and tender. Place the garlic and stir-fry for about 30 seconds, or until aromatic. Transfer to the plate with the pork chops.
6. Pour the light soy, dark soy, red wine vinegar and a pinch of sugar into the wok, and stir to combine well. Bring to a boil and take the onion and pork chops back to the wok. Toss to combine as the sauce starts to thicken slightly. Scoop out the ginger and discard. Transfer to a platter and serve hot.

Beef and Broccoli with Oyster Sauce

Prep Time: 8 minutes, Cook Time: 5 minutes, Serves: 4

INGREDIENTS:

1 pound (454 g) sirloin tips, cut into ¼-inch strips	2 tbsps. cooking oil
1 cup broccoli florets	2 tbsps. Shaoxing rice wine
¼ cup oyster sauce	2 tbsps. soy sauce
2 garlic cloves, crushed and chopped	1 tbsp. ginger, crushed and chopped

DIRECTIONS:

1. In a wok, heat the cooking oil over high heat until it shimmers.
2. Add the garlic and ginger and stir-fry for about 30 seconds until lightly browned.
3. Place the steak, broccoli, rice wine and stir-fry for about 1 minute.
4. Pour in the soy sauce and oyster sauce and stir-fry for about 1 minute.
5. Serve hot.

Ginger Beef and Broccoli

Prep Time: 15 minutes, Cook Time: 20 minutes, Serves: 4

INGREDIENTS:

¾ pound (340 g) skirt steak, cut across the grain into ¼-inch-thick slices	4 tbsps. water, divided
	2 tbsps. vegetable oil
1 pound (454 g) broccoli, cut into bite-size florets	2 tbsps. oyster sauce
	2 tbsps. Shaoxing rice wine
2 garlic cloves, finely minced	2 tsps. light brown sugar
	1 tbsp. baking soda
4 peeled fresh ginger slices, about the size of a quarter	1 tbsp. cornstarch
	1 tbsp. hoisin sauce
	Kosher salt

DIRECTIONS:

1. Mix together the beef and baking soda to coat in a small bowl. Set aside for about 10 minutes. Rinse the beef extremely well and then blot it dry with paper towels.
2. Stir the cornstarch with 2 tbsps. of water and mix in the rice wine, oyster sauce, brown sugar and hoisin sauce in another small bowl. Keep aside.
3. Heat a wok over high heat until a drop of water sizzles and evaporates on contact. Add the oil and swirl to coat the base of the wok well. Season the oil with the ginger and a pinch of salt. Let the ginger sizzle in the oil for 30 seconds, swirling slowly. Place the beef to the wok and stir-fry for about 3 to 4 minutes, until no longer pink. Take the beef to a bowl

and keep aside.
4. Add the garlic and broccoli and stir-fry for about 1 minute, then add the remaining 2 tbsps. of water. Cover the lid and steam the broccoli for about 6 to 8 minutes, until it is crisp-tender.
5. Take the beef back to the wok and stir in the sauce for about 2 to 3 minutes, until completely coated and the sauce has thickened slightly. Scoop out and discard the ginger, then transfer to a platter. Serve hot.

Hoisin Beef Lettuce Cups with Water Chestnuts

Prep Time: 12 minutes, Cook Time: 15 minutes, Serves: 4

INGREDIENTS:

¾ pound (340 g) ground beef	thinly sliced
	2 garlic cloves, finely minced
1 (4-ounce / 113-g) can diced water chestnuts, drained and rinsed	3 tbsps. vegetable oil, divided
8 broad iceberg (or Bibb) lettuce leaves, trimmed to neat round cups	2 tbsps. hoisin sauce
	1 tbsp. peeled finely minced ginger
1 carrot, peeled and julienned	2 tsps. cornstarch
	Kosher salt
3 scallions, white and green parts separated,	Freshly ground black pepper

DIRECTIONS:

1. Sprinkle the beef with the cornstarch and a pinch each of salt and pepper in a bowl. Mix to combine well.
2. Heat a wok over high heat until a bead of water sizzles and evaporates on contact. Add 2 tbsps. of oil and swirl to coat the base of the wok well. Place the beef and brown on both sides, then toss and flip, breaking up the beef into crumbles and clumps for about 3 to 4 minutes, until the beef is no longer pink. Take the beef to a clean bowl and keep aside.
3. Wipe the wok clean and turn it to medium heat. Pour in the remaining 1 tbsp. of oil and quickly stir-fry the garlic and ginger with a pinch of salt. Once the garlic is aromatic, toss in the carrot and water chestnuts for about 2 to 3 minutes, until the carrot turns soft. Turn the heat to medium, take the beef back to the wok, and toss with the hoisin sauce and the scallion whites. Toss to combine well, for about another 45 seconds.
4. Spread out the lettuce leaves, 2 per plate, and evenly distribute the beef mixture among the lettuce leaves. Sprinkle with the scallion greens and eat as you would a soft taco.

Japanese Tamari Pork

Prep Time: 6 minutes, Cook Time: 4 minutes, Serves: 4

INGREDIENTS:

1 pound (454 g) pork tenderloin, cut into 1-inch pieces
2 garlic cloves, crushed and chopped
2 tbsps. cooking oil
2 tbsps. tamari
2 tbsps. ginger, crushed and chopped
2 tbsps. brown sugar
2 tbsps. mirin
2 tbsps. sake
1 tbsp. white miso

DIRECTIONS:

1. Whisk together the miso and tamari in a small bowl. Keep aside.
2. In a wok, heat the cooking oil over high heat until it shimmers.
3. Add the garlic, ginger, pork and sake and stir-fry for about 1 minute.
4. Place the brown sugar and mirin and stir-fry for about 1 minute.
5. Stir in the miso and tamari mixture and toss well.
6. Serve warm.

Sweet Lamb and Cabbage

Prep Time: 7 minutes, Cook Time: 6 minutes, Serves: 5

INGREDIENTS:

1 pound (454 g) boneless leg of lamb or shoulder, cut into ¼-inch strips
1 cup Napa cabbage, shredded
1 medium onion, diced
¼ cup rice vinegar
2 garlic cloves, crushed and chopped
2 tbsps. cooking oil
2 tbsps. brown sugar
2 tbsps. soy sauce
2 tbsps. cornstarch
1 tbsp. ginger, crushed and chopped
1 tsp. red pepper flakes

DIRECTIONS:

1. Whisk together the soy sauce, rice vinegar, brown sugar and cornstarch in a small bowl. Keep aside.
2. In a wok, heat the cooking oil over high heat until it shimmers.
3. Add the garlic, ginger, lamb, onion and red pepper flakes and stir-fry for about 2 minutes.
4. Pour in the soy sauce mixture and cabbage and stir until a glaze is formed.
5. Serve warm.

Myanmarese Curried Lamb

Prep Time: 7 minutes, Cook Time: 5 minutes, Serves: 4

INGREDIENTS:

1 pound (454 g) boneless leg of lamb or rump, sliced into ¼-inch strips against the grain
1 medium onion, cut into ¼-inch pieces
1 chile, cut into ¼-inch rounds
4 garlic cloves, crushed and chopped
4 scallions, cut into 1-inch pieces
2 tbsps. cooking oil
2 tbsps. ginger, crushed and chopped
1 tbsp. brown sugar
1 tbsp. paprika
1 tbsp. soy sauce
1 tbsp. rice vinegar
1 tsp. hot sesame oil

DIRECTIONS:

1. In a wok, heat the cooking oil over high heat until it shimmers.
2. Add the garlic, ginger, onion, paprika and lamb and stir-fry for about 2 minutes.
3. Place the chile, rice vinegar, soy sauce and brown sugar and stir-fry for about 1 minute.
4. Pour in the sesame oil and scallions and toss lightly.
5. Serve warm.

Korean Garlic Pork with Kimchi

Prep Time: 7 minutes, Cook Time: 5 minutes, Serves: 4

INGREDIENTS:

1 pound (454 g) pork tenderloin, cut into 1-inch pieces
½ cup kimchi, cut into ½-inch pieces, drained and juice reserved
¼ cup gochujang
4 scallions, cut into 1-inch pieces
2 garlic cloves, crushed and chopped
2 tbsps. cooking oil
2 tbsps. rice wine
1 tbsp. cornstarch
1 tbsp. ginger, crushed and chopped

DIRECTIONS:

1. Whisk together the kimchi juice, rice wine, gochujang and cornstarch in a small bowl. Set aside.
2. In a wok, heat the cooking oil over high heat until it shimmers.
3. Add the garlic, ginger and pork and stir-fry for about 1 minute.
4. Put the kimchi and stir-fry for about 30 seconds.
5. Pour in the gochujang mixture and stir until a glaze is formed.
6. Sprinkle with the scallions and serve warm.

Thai Pork with Basil

Prep Time: 7 minutes, Cook Time: 5 minutes, Serves: 4

INGREDIENTS:

1 pound (454 g) ground pork	and chopped
1 medium red bell pepper, cut into ½-inch pieces	2 tbsps. cooking oil
	1 tbsp. ginger, crushed and chopped
1 handful fresh Thai basil leaves	1 tbsp. fish sauce
	2 tbsps. brown sugar
2 garlic cloves, crushed	1 tbsp. soy sauce

DIRECTIONS:

1. In a wok, heat the cooking oil over high heat until it shimmers.
2. Add the garlic, ginger and pork and stir-fry for about 2 minutes.
3. Pour the bell pepper, brown sugar, fish sauce and soy sauce and stir-fry for about 1 minute.
4. Sprinkle the basil and stir-fry until just wilted.
5. Serve warm.

Korean Beef Bowl with Kimchi

Prep Time: 8 minutes, Cook Time: 5 minutes, Serves: 4

INGREDIENTS:

1 pound (454 g) ground beef	2 tbsps. cooking oil
	2 tbsps. soy sauce
1 cup kimchi	2 tbsps. gochujang
1 medium onion, diced	1 tbsp. sesame seeds
4 scallions, cut into ½-inch pieces	1 tbsp. ginger, crushed and chopped
2 garlic cloves, crushed and chopped	1 tsp. hot sesame oil

DIRECTIONS:

1. In a wok, heat the cooking oil over high heat until it shimmers.
2. Add the garlic, ginger, beef, soy sauce and onion and stir-fry for about 1 minute.
3. Stir in the kimchi, gochujang and sesame oil and stir-fry for about 1 minute.
4. Sprinkle with the sesame seeds and scallions. Serve warm.

Quick Teriyaki Beef and Pea Pods

Prep Time: 6 minutes, Cook Time: 5 minutes, Serves: 6

INGREDIENTS:

1 pound (454 g) sirloin tips, cut into ¼-inch strips	2 tbsps. tamari
	2 tbsps. mirin
2 cups sugar snap or snow pea pods	2 tbsps. brown sugar
	1 tbsp. ginger, crushed and chopped
2 garlic cloves, crushed and chopped	1 tbsp. cornstarch
2 tbsps. cooking oil	

DIRECTIONS:

1. In a wok, heat the cooking oil over high heat until it shimmers.
2. Add the garlic and ginger and stir-fry for about 30 seconds.
3. Place the steak and tamari and stir-fry for about 1 minute.
4. Put the pea pods and stir-fry for about 1 minute.
5. Toss the sugar, mirin and cornstarch and stir until a light glaze is formed.
6. Serve warm.

Japanese Beef Rice

Prep Time: 10 minutes, Cook Time: 5 minutes, Serves: 4

INGREDIENTS:

1 pound (454 g) shaved steak	½ cup dashi broth
	2 tbsps. cooking oil
1 medium onion, halved and cut into ¼-inch strips	1 tbsp. ginger, crushed and chopped
3 scallions, cut into ½-inch pieces	1 tbsp. sake
	1 tbsp. mirin
2 garlic cloves, crushed and chopped	1 tbsp. sugar
	1 tbsp. tamari

DIRECTIONS:

1. In a wok, heat the cooking oil over high heat until it shimmers.
2. Add the garlic, ginger and onion and stir-fry for about 1 minute.
3. Place the dashi, mirin, tamari, sake and sugar and bring to a boil.
4. Stir in the steak. Put the scallions and stir for about 1 minute.
5. Serve warm.

Pork and Bok Choy with Oyster Sauce

Prep Time: 6 minutes, Cook Time: 5 minutes, Serves: 4

INGREDIENTS:

1 pound (454 g) ground pork
2 cups chopped bok choy
¼ cup oyster sauce
4 scallions, cut into 1-inch pieces
2 garlic cloves, crushed and chopped
2 tbsps. cooking oil
1 tbsp. Chinese five-spice powder
1 tbsp. ginger, crushed and chopped
1 tsp. hot sesame oil

DIRECTIONS:

1. In a wok, heat the cooking oil over high heat until it shimmers.
2. Add the garlic, ginger, pork and five-spice powder and stir-fry for about 1 minute.
3. Place the sesame oil and bok choy and stir-fry for about 1 minute.
4. Pour the oyster sauce, toss with the stir-fry, and sauté for about 30 seconds.
5. Sprinkle with the scallions and serve warm.

Hoisin Pork, Mushrooms and Sugar Snap

Prep Time: 12 minutes, Cook Time: 5 minutes, Serves: 6

INGREDIENTS:

1 pound (454 g) pork tenderloin, cut into 1-inch pieces
2 cups sugar snap or snow pea pods
1 medium onion, cut into 1-inch pieces
4 ounces (113 g) sliced mushrooms
4 scallions, cut into 1-inch pieces
2 garlic cloves, crushed and chopped
¼ cup hoisin sauce
2 tbsps. cooking oil
2 tbsps. soy sauce
1 tbsp. ginger, crushed and chopped

DIRECTIONS:

1. In a wok, heat the cooking oil over high heat until it shimmers.
2. Add the garlic, ginger and pork and stir-fry for about 1 minute.
3. Place the onion, mushrooms and pea pods and stir-fry for about 1 minute.
4. Put the hoisin sauce and soy sauce and stir-fry for about 30 seconds.
5. Sprinkle with the scallions and serve warm.

Vietnamese Caramelized Pork with Kimchi

Prep Time: 9 minutes, Cook Time: 5 minutes, Serves: 4

INGREDIENTS:

1 pound (454 g) ground pork
½ cup chopped kimchi
1 medium onion, diced
¼ cup brown sugar
4 scallions, cut into ½-inch pieces
2 garlic cloves, crushed
and chopped
2 tbsps. coconut oil
1 tbsp. ginger, crushed and chopped
1 tbsp. fish sauce
1 tsp. ground black pepper

DIRECTIONS:

1. In a wok, heat the coconut oil over high heat until it shimmers.
2. Add the garlic, ginger, onion and pork and stir-fry for about 2 minutes.
3. Place the fish sauce, black pepper and brown sugar and stir-fry for about 1 minute.
4. Put the kimchi and stir-fry for about 30 seconds.
5. Top with the scallions and serve hot.

Lime Beef

Prep Time: 8 minutes, Cook Time: 6 minutes, Serves: 4

INGREDIENTS:

1 pound (454 g) sirloin steak, sliced into ¼-inch strips
1 chile, cut into ¼-inch rounds
Juice of 1 lime
1 lemongrass heart (the bottom 2 inches of the white inner layers), minced
4 scallions, cut into ½-inch pieces
2 garlic cloves, crushed and chopped
2 tbsps. coconut oil
2 tbsps. soy sauce
1 tbsp. ginger, crushed and chopped
1 tbsp. brown sugar
1 tsp. Chinese five-spice powder
1 tsp. cardamom

DIRECTIONS:

1. In a wok, heat the coconut oil over high heat until it shimmers.
2. Add the garlic, ginger, steak, five-spice powder and cardamom and stir-fry for about 2 minutes.
3. Place the chile, lime juice, brown sugar, lemongrass and soy sauce and stir-fry for about 2 minutes.
4. Sprinkle with the scallions and serve warm.

Sriracha Pork and Eggplant

Prep Time: 11 minutes, Cook Time: 5 minutes, Serves: 5

INGREDIENTS:

1 pound (454 g) ground pork
1 small eggplant, diced into ½-inch cubes
2 chiles, cut into ¼-inch circles (no need to core or seed)
¼ cup sriracha

4 scallions, cut into 1-inch pieces
2 garlic cloves, crushed and chopped
2 tbsps. cooking oil
2 tbsps. hoisin sauce
1 tbsp. ginger, crushed and chopped

DIRECTIONS:

1. In a wok, heat the cooking oil over high heat until it shimmers.
2. Add the garlic, ginger and eggplant and stir-fry for about 1 minute.
3. Place the pork and stir-fry for about 2 minutes.
4. Toss the sriracha, chiles and hoisin sauce and stir-fry for about 1 minute.
5. Top with the scallions and serve warm.

Pork and Brussels Sprouts with Oyster Sauce

Prep Time: 12 minutes, Cook Time: 5 minutes, Serves: 4

INGREDIENTS:

1 pound (454 g) ground pork
1 dozen Brussels sprouts, trimmed and halved
1 medium onion, diced
¼ cup honey

¼ cup oyster sauce
2 garlic cloves, crushed and chopped
2 tbsps. cooking oil
1 tbsp. ginger, crushed and chopped

DIRECTIONS:

1. In a wok, heat the cooking oil over high heat until it shimmers.
2. Add the garlic, ginger and brussels sprouts and stir-fry for about 1 minute.
3. Place the pork, onion and honey and stir-fry for about 2 minutes.
4. Put the oyster sauce and toss for about 30 seconds.
5. Serve warm.

Honey Shrimp with Walnut, page 82

Shrimp and Water Chestnuts Dumplings, page 83

Steamed Egg Custard with Scallion, page 82

Steamed Mango Milk Custard, page 83

Chapter 12: Snack and Dessert

Garlic Kimchi Chicken and Cabbage

Prep Time: 8 minutes, Cook Time: 5 minutes, Serves: 4

INGREDIENTS:

1 pound (454 g) ground chicken
1 cup chopped kimchi
2 heads baby bok choy, leaves separated
2 garlic cloves, crushed and chopped
2 tbsps. cooking oil
2 tbsps. sesame seeds
1 tbsp. ginger, crushed and chopped
1 tbsp. fish sauce
1 tbsp. gochujang
1 tbsp. toasted sesame oil

DIRECTIONS:

1. In a wok, heat the cooking oil over high heat until it shimmers.
2. Add the garlic, ginger, and chicken and stir-fry for about 2 minutes.
3. Put the kimchi, bok choy, gochujang and fish sauce and stir-fry for about 1 minute.
4. Pour in the sesame oil and sesame seeds and toss.
5. Serve hot.

Honey-Garlic Chicken and Broccoli

Prep Time: 12 minutes, Cook Time: 6 minutes, Serves: 4

INGREDIENTS:

1 pound (454 g) boneless chicken thighs, cut into 1-inch pieces
1 cup broccoli florets, cut into bite-size pieces
1 medium carrot, roll-cut into ½-inch pieces
1 medium onion, cut into 1-inch pieces
1 red bell pepper, cut into 1-inch pieces
4 scallions, cut into 1-inch pieces
3 garlic cloves, crushed and chopped
2 tbsps. cooking oil
2 tbsps. soy sauce
2 tbsps. honey
1 tbsp. cornstarch
1 tbsp. ginger, crushed and chopped

DIRECTIONS:

1. Whisk together the soy sauce, honey, and cornstarch in a small bowl. Keep aside.
2. In a wok, heat the cooking oil over high heat until it shimmers.
3. Add the garlic, ginger, carrot and chicken and stir-fry for about 2 minutes.
4. Place the onion and stir-fry for about 1 minute.
5. Put the broccoli and bell pepper and stir-fry for about 1 minute.
6. Pour soy sauce mixture to the wok and stir until a glaze is formed.
7. Sprinkle with the scallions and serve warm.

Quick Sugar Egg Puffs

Prep Time: 10 minutes, Cook Time: 20 minutes, Makes: 8 puffs

INGREDIENTS:

3 cups vegetable oil
2 large eggs, beaten
½ cup water
½ cup all-purpose
unbleached flour
¼ cup sugar, divided
2 tsps. unsalted butter
Kosher salt

DIRECTIONS:

1. In a small saucepan over medium-high heat, heat the water, butter, 2 tsps. of sugar, and a pinch of salt. Bring to a boil and stir in the flour. Use a wooden spoon to continue stirring the flour until the mixture looks like mashed potatoes and a thin film of dough has developed on the bottom of the pan. Remove from the heat and transfer the dough to a large mixing bowl. Cool the dough for 5 minutes, stirring from time to time.
2. While the dough cools, add the oil thet should be about 1 to 1½ inches deep into the wok. Bring the oil over medium-high heat to 375ºF (190ºC). When you dip the end of a wooden spoon in and the oil bubbles and sizzles around the spoon, you can tell the oil is ready.
3. Pour the beaten eggs into the dough in two batches, vigorously stirring the eggs into the dough before placing the next batch. When all the eggs have been incorporated, the batter should become satiny and shiny.
4. Using 2 tablespoons, scoop the batter with one and use the other to lightly nudge the batter off the spoon into the hot oil. Allow the puffs to fry for about 8 to 10 minutes, flipping frequently, until the puffs swell to 3 times their original size and turn golden brown and crispy.
5. Transfer the puffs to a paper towel–lined plate with a wok skimmer, and cool for about 2 to 3 minutes. Add the remaining sugar in a bowl and toss the puffs in it. Serve hot.

Hoisin Sesame Tofu

Prep Time: 5 minutes, Cook Time: 5 minutes, Serves: 2 to 4

INGREDIENTS:

SAUCE:
2 tsps. sesame oil
2 tbsps. hoisin sauce
1 tbsp. honey
1 tsp. soy sauce
STIR-FRY:

1 block firm tofu, cut into
1- to 1½-inch cubes
1 scallion, chopped
2 tbsps. peanut oil
1 tsp. toasted sesame
seeds

DIRECTIONS:
1. Make the sauce by combining the hoisin sauce, honey, sesame oil and soy sauce in a small bowl. Keep aside.
2. In a wok, heat the peanut oil over medium-high heat.
3. Gently drop the tofu cubes into the wok, and let the bottom side cook for 20 seconds before slowly flipping them over.
4. Once the tofu is cooked on all sides, top with the sauce, slowly stirring to coat the tofu cubes.
5. Take the tofu to a serving plate. Sprinkle with the sesame seeds and chopped scallion. Serve warm.

Chicken and Black Beans Tacos

Prep Time: 20 minutes, Cook Time: 45 minutes, Serves: 12

INGREDIENTS:

1 pound (454 g) boneless chicken, cut into ¾-inch cubes
1 (16-ounce / 454-g) package yellow rice
1 (16-ounce / 454-g) can black beans, rinsed and drained
12 corn tortillas
1½ cups shredded Mexican cheese blend
4 cups water

1 (4-ounce / 113-g) can sliced olives
1 (1-ounce / 28-g) package chicken taco seasoning mix
1 jalapeño pepper, seeded and minced
5 tbsps. olive oil, divided (optional)
1 tbsp. vegetable shortening

DIRECTIONS:
1. In a pan over high heat, add the water and bring to a boil.
2. Place the rice and ¼ cup of the olive oil and bring to a boil.
3. Turn the heat to medium-low and simmer, covered for 20 to 25 minutes.
4. In a wok over medium heat, heat 1 tbsp. of the olive oil and stir fry the chicken and taco seasoning mix for 5 to 10 minutes.

5. Stir in the rice, black beans, olives, Mexican cheese blend and jalapeño pepper and cook for 5 minutes.
6. In another wok on medium-high heat, warm each tortillas for 1 to 2 minutes.
7. Fill each tortilla with about ½ cup of the chicken mixture, gently folding tortilla over filling.
8. In a wok on medium heat, heat the shortening and fry the filled tortillas for 2 to 3 minutes per side. Serve warm.

Crab Egg Foo Young Patties

Prep Time: 8 minutes, Cook Time: 17 minutes, Serves: 4 to 6

INGREDIENTS:

SAUCE:
1 tbsp. oyster sauce
1 cup chicken stock
2 tsps. cornstarch
2 tsps. soy sauce
½ tsp. sesame oil
MARINADE:
1 tsp. soy sauce
4 eggs
½ tsp. salt
Pinch ground white

pepper
EGG FOO YOUNG:
1 cup cooked crab meat
2 cups fresh bean sprouts
½ small yellow onion, diced
½ cup chopped scallion
4 tbsps. peanut oil, divided
1 tbsp. water

DIRECTIONS:
1. Prepare the sauce by combining the chicken stock, oyster sauce, soy sauce, cornstarch and sesame oil in a small bowl. Keep aside.
2. Season the eggs with the soy sauce, salt and pepper in a separate bowl. Beat lightly until well combined.
3. In a wok, heat 1 tbsp. of peanut oil over medium heat.
4. Place the onion and stir-fry until translucent.
5. Pour the fresh bean sprouts and water to the wok, and stir-fry for 20 seconds.
6. When all the water has evaporated and the bean sprouts have softened a little, place the crab meat and scallions. Remove from the heat and transfer the crab mixture to a large bowl.
7. Add the eggs over the crab mixture and stir to combine well.
8. In the wok over medium-high heat, heat the remaining 3 tbsps. of peanut oil.
9. Add about ⅓ cup of the egg-crab mixture into the wok. Cook until golden brown, or for 2 minutes on each side. Keep aside. Repeat this with the remaining mixture, ⅓ cup at a time.
10. Stir the sauce well and pour it into the wok. Simmer until the sauce thickens, then scoop the sauce over the egg foo young patties. Serve warm.

Soft Steamed Scallion Buns

Prep Time: 90 minutes, Cook Time: 20 minutes, Makes: 8 buns

INGREDIENTS:

2 cups all-purpose flour
¾ cup whole milk, at room temperature
6 scallions, thinly sliced
2 tbsps. sesame oil, divided
1 tbsp. sugar
2 tsps. Chinese five spice powder, divided
1 tsp. active dry yeast
1 tsp. baking powder
¾ tsp. kosher salt, divided

DIRECTIONS:

1. Stir together the milk, sugar and yeast in a liquid measuring cup. Keep aside for about 5 minutes to activate the yeast.
2. In a large mixing bowl or using a stand mixer with a dough hook attachment on low, stir the baking powder, flour and ¼ tsp. of salt to combine well. Pour in the milk mixture and mix for about 30 seconds. Increase the speed to high and mix for about 5 minutes, until a soft, elastic dough forms, or 6 to 8 minutes by hand. Turn the dough out onto a work surface and use hand to knead a few times until smooth. Place in a bowl and cover with a towel to rest for about 10 minutes.
3. Slice the dough in half. Roll one piece out into a rectangle, 15 by 18 inches with a rolling pin. Brush 1 tbsp. of sesame oil over the dough. Sprinkle with 1 tsp. of five spice powder and ¼ tsp. of salt. Scatter with half the scallions and press lightly into the dough.
4. As you would a cinnamon roll, roll the dough up starting from the long edge. Cut the rolled log into 8 equal pieces. To shape the bun, take 2 pieces and stack them one on top of the other on their sides, so the cut sides are facing out.
5. Press down in the center of the stack with a chopstick; this will push out the filling slightly. Take the chopstick. Pull the two ends of the dough out slightly to stretch with your fingers, and then coil the ends underneath the middle, pinching the ends together.
6. Put the bun on a 3-inch square of parchment paper and place inside a steamer basket to proof. Repeat the shaping process with the remaining dough, making sure there is at least 2 inches of space between the buns. If you need more room, you can use a second steamer basket. You should have 8 twisted buns. Use plastic wrap to cover the baskets and let rise for about 1 hour, or until doubled in size.
7. Pour 2 inches of water into the wok and put the steamer baskets in the wok. The water level should come above the bottom rim of the steamer by ¼ to ½ inch but not so high that it touches the bottom of the basket. Use the steamer basket lid to cover the baskets and bring the water to a boil over medium-high heat.
8. Turn the heat to medium and steam for about 15 minutes, pouring more water to the wok if needed. Remove from the heat and keep the baskets covered for about 5 more minutes. Take the buns to a platter and serve warm.

Baked Beef Burritos

Prep Time: 13 minutes, Cook Time: 18 minutes, Serves: 6

INGREDIENTS:

1 pound (454 g) ground beef
6 (12 inch) flour tortillas, warmed
1 (4½-ounce / 128-g) can diced green chile peppers
1 (16-ounce / 454-g) can refried beans
1 (15-ounce / 425-g) can chili without beans
1 (10¾-ounce / 305-g) can condensed tomato soup
1 (10-ounce / 283-g) can enchilada sauce
2 cups shredded lettuce
2 cups shredded Mexican blend cheese
1 cup chopped tomatoes
½ cup chopped onion
½ cup chopped green onions
1 clove garlic, minced
½ tsp. cumin
¼ tsp. salt
⅛ tsp. pepper

DIRECTIONS:

1. In a large wok on medium-high heat, cook the beef until browned completely.
2. Add the onion and cook until translucent.
3. Drain the grease from the wok.
4. In the wok over high heat, place the cumin, garlic, salt, pepper, green chilies and refried beans and stir until well combined.
5. Remove from the heat but keep the wok, covered on stove to make the mixture warm.
6. In a wok on medium heat, mix together the chili without beans, tomato soup and enchilada sauce and cook until heated fully.
7. Remove from the heat but keep the wok, covered on stove to make the mixture warm.
8. Put each warmed tortilla onto a plate.
9. Add about ½ cup of the beef mixture in the center of each tortilla and top with lettuce and tomato. Roll up the tortillas over the filling tightly.
10. Pour a generous amount of the sauce over each tortilla and scatter with the cheese and green onions.
11. Put the tortillas onto a microwave safe plate and microwave for 30 seconds. Serve warm.

Chrysanthemum and Yellow Peach Tong Sui

Prep Time: 5 minutes, Cook Time: 15 minutes, Serves: 4

INGREDIENTS:

2 large yellow peaches, peeled, pitted, and sliced into 8 wedges each
¾ cup granulated sugar
¼ cup light brown sugar
3 cups water
2-inch fresh ginger piece, peeled and smashed
1 tbsp. dried chrysanthemum buds

DIRECTIONS:

1. In a wok, bring the water to a boil over high heat, then turn the heat to medium-low and place the granulated sugar, ginger, brown sugar and chrysanthemum buds. Stir lightly to dissolve the sugars. Put the peaches.
2. Simmer lightly for about 10 to 15 minutes, or until the peaches are soft. They may impart a beautiful rosy color to the soup. Remove and discard the ginger. Distribute the soup and peaches into bowls and serve warm.

Quick Drunken Shrimp

Prep Time: 30 minutes, Cook Time: 10 minutes, Serves: 4

INGREDIENTS:

1 pound (454 g) jumbo shrimp, peeled and deveined, tails left on
2 cups Shaoxing rice wine
4 peeled fresh ginger slices, each about the
size of a quarter
2 tbsps. vegetable oil
2 tbsps. dried goji berries (optional)
2 tsps. sugar
2 tsps. cornstarch
Kosher salt

DIRECTIONS:

1. Stir together the rice wine, ginger, goji berries (if using) and sugar in a wide mixing bowl, until the sugar is dissolved. Place the shrimp and cover. Marinate in the refrigerator for about 20 to 30 minutes.
2. Pour the shrimp and marinade into a colander set over a bowl. Reserve ½ cup of the marinade and discard the rest.
3. Heat a wok over high heat until a drop of water sizzles and evaporates on contact. Add the oil and swirl to coat the base of the wok well. Season the oil with a small pinch of salt, and swirl slowly.
4. Place the shrimp and vigorously stir-fry, putting a pinch of salt as you flip and toss the shrimp around in the wok. Keep moving the shrimp around for 3 minutes, until they just become pink.

5. Stir the cornstarch into the reserved marinade and pour it over the shrimp. Toss the shrimp and coat with the marinade evenly. It will thicken into a glossy sauce as it begins to boil, for another 5 minutes more.
6. Take the shrimp and goji berries to a platter, remove and discard the ginger. Serve hot.

Steamed Cabbage and Carrot Dumplings

Prep Time: 16 minutes, Cook Time: 10 minutes, Makes: 15 to 20 dumplings

INGREDIENTS:
DUMPLINGS:
15 to 20 round wonton wrappers
4 cups shredded cabbage
1 carrot, shredded
5 to 8 garlic chives, cut into 1-inch pieces
2 scallions, chopped
1-inch piece of ginger, peeled and minced
1 tbsp. water
2 tsps. olive oil
2 tsps. sesame oil, plus 2 tsps. for brushing
Salt
Pepper
DIPPING SAUCE:
1-inch piece of ginger, peeled and finely minced
2 tsps. sesame oil
2 tbsps. soy sauce
2 tsps. rice vinegar
1 tsp. chili oil

DIRECTIONS:

1. In a wok, heat the olive oil over medium heat.
2. Place the cabbage, carrot, garlic chives, scallions and ginger to the wok. Stir-fry for 1 minute.
3. Pour the water to help steam the vegetables. Stir-fry until most of the water has evaporated. Add 2 tsps. of sesame oil over the vegetables. Season with salt and pepper to taste, and toss well. Turn off the heat and keep it aside to cool.
4. Put about 1 tsp. of vegetable mixture in the middle of a wonton wrapper.
5. Dampen the edges of the wonton wrapper with a little water, gently fold the wrapper in half so that it forms a triangle, and slowly press down to seal the edges.
6. Brush the dumplings with a light coating of sesame oil.
7. Gently line a bamboo steamer with parchment paper liners. Place the dumplings on top and steam for about 8 minutes, or until the wonton wrappers turn slightly translucent.
8. While the dumplings are steaming, make the dipping sauce. In a small bowl, combine the soy sauce, sesame oil, chili oil, rice vinegar and ginger.
9. Serve the dumplings with the dipping sauce.

Appetizer Bok Choy

Prep Time: 6 minutes, Cook Time: 25 minutes, Serves: 3

INGREDIENTS:

1 pound (454 g) baby bok choy, trimmed and sliced in half lengthwise	1 cup white wine
	3 tbsps. butter
	1 clove garlic, smashed
2 cups chicken stock	1 bay leaf

DIRECTIONS:

1. In a large wok over medium heat, melt the butter and cook the garlic and bay leaf for 5 minutes.
2. Toss in the chicken stock and white wine, and bring to a full boil.
3. Cook for 15 minutes, stirring constantly.
4. Remove and discard the bay leaf.
5. Put the bok choy halves, cut sides down into the sauce and reduce heat.
6. Simmer for 10 minutes.
7. Add the sauce over the bok choy and serve hot.

Sweet Tea-Soaked Eggs

Prep Time: 5 minutes, Cook Time: 40 minutes, Serves: 4

INGREDIENTS:

8 large eggs, at room temperature	6 whole cloves
5 decaf black tea bags	2 whole star anise
2 cups water	2 cinnamon sticks
6 peeled fresh ginger slices, each about the size of a quarter	1 tsp. sugar
	1 tsp. fennel seeds
	1 tsp. Sichuan peppercorns or black peppercorns
¾ cup dark soy sauce	

DIRECTIONS:

1. In a saucepan over high heat, bring the water to a boil. Place the dark soy, ginger, anise, cinnamon sticks, cloves, peppercorns, fennel seeds and sugar. Cover the pot, turn the heat to a simmer and cook for about 20 minutes. Remove from the heat and add the tea bags. Steep the tea for about 10 minutes. Through a fine-mesh sieve, strain the tea into a large heatproof measuring cup and let cool while you cook the eggs.
2. Create an ice bath for the eggs by filling a large bowl with ice and water and set aside. In a wok over high heat, bring enough water to cover the eggs by about an inch to a boil. Slowly lower the eggs into the water, reduce the heat to a simmer, and cook for about 9 minutes. Use a slotted spoon to remove the eggs and transfer to the ice bath until cool.
3. Take the eggs from the ice bath. Use the back of a spoon to tap the eggs to crack the shells so the

marinade can seep in between the cracks, but lighty enough to leave the shells on. The shells should end up looking like a mosaic. Put the eggs in a large jar (at least 32 ounces / 907 g) and cover them with the marinade. Remove the eggs from the marinade when ready to serve.

Almond Sponge Cake

Prep Time: 10 minutes, Cook Time: 25 minutes, Serves: 4

INGREDIENTS:

Nonstick cooking spray	1 tsp. baking powder
5 large eggs, separated	1 tsp. almond extract
1 cup cake flour, sifted	½ tsp. cream of tartar
¾ cup sugar, divided	¼ tsp. kosher salt

DIRECTIONS:

1. Gently line an 8-inch cake pan with parchment paper. Spray the parchment with nonstick cooking spray and keep aside.
2. Sift the cake flour, baking powder, and salt together into a bowl.
3. Beat the egg yolks with ½ cup of sugar and the almond extract for about 3 minutes in a stand mixer or hand mixer on medium, until pale and thick. Place the flour mixture and mix until just combined. Keep aside.
4. Clean the whisk and whip the egg whites with the cream of tartar until frothy in another clean bowl. While the mixer is running, continue to whisk the whites while slowly adding the remaining ¼ cup of sugar. Beat for about 4 to 5 minutes, until the whites becomes shiny and develop stiff peaks.
5. Gently fold the egg whites into the cake batter and lightly combine until the egg whites are incorporated. Take the batter to the prepared cake pan.
6. Rinse a bamboo steamer basket and its lid with cold water and place it in the wok. Add 2 inches of water, or until it comes above the bottom rim of the steamer by ¼ to ½ inch, but not so much that it touches the bottom of the basket. Arrange the center pan in the steamer basket.
7. Bring the water to a boil over high heat. Put the cover on the steamer basket and low the heat down to medium. Steam the cake for about 25 minutes, or until a toothpick inserted into the center comes out clean.
8. Take the cake to a wire cooling rack and cool for about 10 minutes. Turn the cake out onto the rack and take the parchment paper. Invert the cake back onto a serving plate so that it is right side up. Cut into 8 wedges and serve warm.

Steamed Egg Custard with Scallion

Prep Time: 6 minutes, Cook Time: 10 minutes, Serves: 4

INGREDIENTS:

4 large eggs, at room temperature
2 scallions, green part only, thinly sliced
1¾ cups low-sodium

chicken broth or filtered water
4 tsps. sesame oil
2 tsps. Shaoxing rice wine

DIRECTIONS:

1. Whisk the eggs in a large bowl. Pour the broth and rice wine and whisk to combine well. Through a fine-mesh sieve set over a liquid measuring cup, strain the egg mixture to remove air bubbles. Pour the egg mixture into 4 (6-ounce / 170-g) ramekins. Pop any bubbles on the surface of the egg mixture with a paring knife. Cover the ramekins with aluminum foil.
2. Rinse a bamboo steamer basket and its lid with cold water and put it in the wok. Add 2 inches of water, or until it comes above the bottom rim of the steamer by ¼ to ½ inch, but not so much that it touches the bottom of the basket. Arrange the ramekins in the steamer basket. Use the lid to cover.
3. Bring the water to a boil, then turn the heat to a low simmer. Steam over low heat for 10 minutes or until the eggs are just set.
4. Gently remove the ramekins from the steamer and sprinkle each custard with some scallions and a few drops of sesame oil. Serve hot.

Japanese Cumin Chicken Stir Fry

Prep Time: 17 minutes, Cook Time: 15 minutes, Serves: 8

INGREDIENTS:

1 (3-pound / 1.4-kg) whole chicken, cut into pieces
⅔ cup soy sauce
¼ cup mirin
1 clove garlic, crushed

3 tbsps. white sugar
2 tbsps. cooking oil
1 tbsp. grated fresh ginger root
1 tbsp. sake

DIRECTIONS:

1. Clean the chicken and pat it dry with a paper towel.
2. Mix the ginger, garlic, sugar, soy sauce, sake and mirin in a glass oven pan. Add the chicken pieces and stir them to coat evenly.
3. Cover the dish with a plastic wrap and put it in the fridge for about 2 hours to 8 hours.
4. In a large wok over medium heat, heat the oil. Drain the chicken pieces from the marinade and fry them until they turn golden brown.
5. Drain the chicken pieces and set them aside. Take

the grease from the pan. Pour the marinade from the chicken into the wok with the browned chicken pieces.
6. Turn the heat to low and cover the lid. Cook the marinade for about 9 minutes to make the sauce. Open the lid and keep cooking them until the chicken is done fully and the sauce is thick.
7. Serve your saucy chicken hot.

Honey Shrimp with Walnut

Prep Time: 35 minutes, Cook Time: 5 minutes, Serves: 4 to 6

INGREDIENTS:

SHRIMP MARINADE:
1 pound (454 g) shrimp, peeled and deveined
2 tsps. baking soda
Pinch salt
Pinch ground white pepper
WALNUTS:
½ cup walnuts
¼ cup sugar

¼ cup water
SAUCE:
1½ tbsps. mayonnaise
1 tsp. sweetened condensed milk
1 tsp. honey
½ tsp. lemon juice
STIR-FRY:
2 tbsps. peanut oil
3 tsps. cornstarch

DIRECTIONS:

1. Add the baking soda over the shrimp and slowly massage it into the shrimp. Let the shrimp rest in the refrigerator for about 30 minutes, then thoroughly wash off the baking soda. Blot any excess water from the shrimp with a paper towel. Season with the salt and pepper.
2. While the shrimp is marinating in the cornstarch, add the sugar and water into a wok over medium-high heat. Stir until the syrup looks a light caramel color. Pour in the walnuts, stirring to coat evenly. After 1 minute, place the walnuts onto parchment paper or aluminum foil and spread them evenly with a wok spatula. Allow them to cool.
3. Prepare the sauce by combining the mayonnaise, honey, condensed milk and lemon juice in a small bowl. Keep it aside.
4. In a wok, heat the peanut oil over medium-high heat.
5. Dredge the shrimp in the cornstarch, shake off the excess, and put them in the wok in a single layer. Cook for 1 minute on one side, then stir-fry until they are completely cooked and take them to a bowl.
6. Place the candied walnuts to the shrimp, followed by the sauce, stirring to coat evenly.
7. Serve hot.

Shrimp and Water Chestnuts Dumplings

Prep Time: 45 minutes, Cook Time: 10 minutes, Makes: 15 to 20 dumplings

INGREDIENTS:
FILLING:
1 pound (454 g) peeled and deveined shrimp, roughly chopped
¼ cup diced water chestnuts
2 tbsps. cornstarch
2 tbsps. finely chopped
fresh cilantro (optional)
1½ tbsps. sesame oil
2 tsps. soy sauce
WRAPPERS:
1¼ cups wheat starch
1¼ cups boiling water
2 tbsps. tapioca flour
1 tsp. peanut oil

DIRECTIONS:
MAKE THE FILLING:
1. Combine the shrimp, water chestnuts, sesame oil, soy sauce and cornstarch in a large bowl. Add the cilantro (if using) and mix well.
2. Marinate the mixture for at least 30 minutes in the refrigerator.
MAKE THE WRAPPERS:
3. Combine the wheat starch and tapioca flour in a large bowl.
4. Gently pour the boiling water into the flour mixture while stirring, until it starts to form a ball of dough.
5. Cover the bowl with a damp towel and let the dough cool down slightly before handling.
6. Use a bit of peanut oil to cover your palms, a small rolling pin and a cutting board for preventing the dough from sticking.
7. Knead the dough for about 2 to 3 minutes.
8. Take about a tsp. of dough and slowly roll it into a ball.
9. Roll the dough out into a small pancake, about 3 inches in diameter.
MAKE THE DUMPLINGS:
10. Place a bamboo steamer in a wok. Line the steamer with parchment paper liners.
11. Put about 1 tsp. of shrimp filling in the middle of a wrapper.
12. Make pleats on one side of the wrapper, then gently fold the other side of the wrapper toward the pleated side to seal the dumpling.
13. Repeat this with the remaining filling and wrappers.
14. Arrange the dumplings in the bamboo steamer and steam for 5 minutes or until cooked through. Serve warm.

Steamed Mango Milk Custard

Prep Time: 5 minutes, Cook Time: 30 minutes, Serves: 4

INGREDIENTS:
3 large egg whites
1 ripe mango, seeded and diced
1¼ cups whole milk
1 cup half-and-half
⅓ cup sugar
1 tsp. vanilla extract

DIRECTIONS:
1. In a medium saucepan over medium heat, stir together the milk, half-and-half, and sugar. Warm the mixture, stirring from time to time, until the sugar has dissolved entirely, for 5 minutes. Do not let the mixture boil or simmer. Remove from the heat and stir in the vanilla. Keep aside.
2. Beat the egg whites until frothy in a mixing bowl. Continue whisking while gently pouring in the milk and stir to combine well.
3. Through a fine-mesh strainer, pour the custard into another bowl and then divide the custard among 4 (6-ounce / 170-g) ramekins or custard cups. Use aluminum foil to cover the ramekins.
4. Rinse a bamboo steamer basket and its lid with cold water and put it in the wok. Add 2 inches of water, or until it comes above the bottom rim of the steamer by ¼ to ½ inch, but not so much that it touches the bottom of the basket. Arrange the ramekins in the steamer basket.
5. Cover the basket and steam over medium-high heat for about 8 minutes. Remove from the heat and allow the custards to sit in place for 10 minutes more before removing from the steamer. The custards will appear set, with a slight wobble.
6. Take the custards to a cooling rack and cool to room temperature before chilling in the refrigerator to set. Top with diced mango and serve chilled.

Appendix 1: Measurement Conversion Chart

Volume Equivalents (Dry)

US STANDARD	METRIC (APPROXIMATE)
1/8 teaspoon	0.5 mL
1/4 teaspoon	1 mL
1/2 teaspoon	2 mL
3/4 teaspoon	4 mL
1 teaspoon	5 mL
1 tablespoon	15 mL
1/4 cup	59 mL
1/2 cup	118 mL
3/4 cup	177 mL
1 cup	235 mL
2 cups	475 mL
3 cups	700 mL
4 cups	1 L

Temperatures Equivalents

FAHRENHEIT (F)	CELSIUS(C) (APPROXIMATE)
225 °F	107 °C
250 °F	120 °C
275 °F	135 °C
300 °F	150 °C
325 °F	160 °C
350 °F	180 °C
375 °F	190 °C
400 °F	205 °C
425 °F	220 °C
450 °F	235 °C
475 °F	245 °C
500 °F	260 °C

Volume Equivalents (Liquid)

US STANDARD	US STANDARD (OUNCES)	METRIC (APPROXIMATE)
2 tablespoons	1 fl.oz.	30 mL
1/4 cup	2 fl.oz.	60 mL
1/2 cup	4 fl.oz.	120 mL
1 cup	8 fl.oz.	240 mL
1 1/2 cup	12 fl.oz.	355 mL
2 cups or 1 pint	16 fl.oz.	475 mL
4 cups or 1 quart	32 fl.oz.	1 L
1 gallon	128 fl.oz.	4 L

Weight Equivalents

US STANDARD	METRIC (APPROXIMATE)
1 ounce	28 g
2 ounces	57 g
5 ounces	142 g
10 ounces	284 g
15 ounces	425 g
16 ounces (1 pound)	455 g
1.5 pounds	680 g
2 pounds	907 g

Appendix 2: Recipes Index

Don't forget to get a free PDF with color pictures!

Getting it is easy, just take out your phone, scan the QR code below! Your PDF is available and will be displayed in color.

To bring you a better shopping experience, we are always working hard. This is the only way we can send you recipes with color pictures and make the book as affordable as possible.

Once you've downloaded the PDF file with your phone, you can take it with you, which means you can cook these recipes anywhere!

We hope you enjoy and let us know your feedback! If you have any questions, or have anything you would like to say to us, please send us an email to healthyrecipegroup@outlook.com and we will be happy to help you! Your satisfaction is our greatest pursuit!

Made in the USA
Las Vegas, NV
25 September 2023